Outline Studies in
JOHN

D1557272

Robert Lee Outline Studies Series

Outline Studies in JOHN

Outline Studies in ACTS

Outline Studies in ROMANS

Outline Studies in GALATIANS

Outline Studies in
JOHN

ROBERT LEE

KREGEL PUBLICATIONS
Grand Rapids, Michigan 49501

Outline Studies in John by Robert Lee. Copyright © 1987 by Kregel Publications, a division of Kregel, Inc. All rights reserved.

Library of Congress Cataloging-in-Publication Data

Lee, Robert, 1872-1956.
  Outline Studies in John.

  Reprint. Originally published: The Outlined John. London: Pickering & Inglis, 1929.
    1. Bible. N.T. John—Sermons—Outlines, syllabi, etc.
I. Title.
BS2615.L32   1987   252'.02   87-3623
ISBN 0-8254-3140-9

1 2 3 4 5 Printing/Year 91 90 89 88 87

Printed in the United States of America

CONTENTS

6   Contents

Contents 7

SECTION 2   LIGHT SHINING
JOHN 13:1—17:26

8 Contents

SECTION 3   LOVE'S   TRIUMPH

JOHN 18:1—20:29

EPILOGUE   CHRIST AND HIS OWN

JOHN 21:1-25

PUBLISHER'S PREFACE

Personal and group Bible studies are becoming very popular. It is encouraging to know that Christians — and non-Christians — are taking seriously the study of God's Word. And a good way to get a better understanding of the Bible is to study it book by book!

The *Robert Lee Outline Studies Series* is an excellent study guide to help you discover various books of the Bible. They will help you obtain a better knowledge of God's Word and give you direction in applying it to your life. The expositional outlines, practical notes and illustrations give insights into each passage studied. Preachers and teachers will also find these outlines helpful in their sermon and lesson preparation.

The abbreviations used refer to the following translations: A.V. = Authorized or King James Version; C. & H. = Conybeare and Howson; J. N. D. = Darby's New Testament; M. = Moffatt's translation; R. = *Rotherham's Emphasized Bible*; R.V. = Revised Version; 20 C. = *Twentieth Century New Testament*; W. = Weymouth's *New Testament in Modern Speech*; and Y. = Young's translation.

PROLOGUE

THE DIVINE WORD

JOHN 1:1-18

THE WORD OF GOD

The Writer's Parents. This book was written by a son of a master fisherman named Zebedee (Matt. 4. 21 ; Mark 1. 19, 20), his mother's name being Salome (Matt. 27. 55, 56 ; Mark 15. 40, 41).

Date When Written. It was the last book but one to be written of all the inspired writings, being written on the Isle of Patmos, and published at Ephesus fifty years after the ascension of Christ.

John's Descriptive Term. John at once introduces us to a Being whom he styles THE WORD. He uses the term without apology or explanation. As a matter of fact the Gentiles would understand of whom the evangelist referred, for they used a similar phrase when speaking of their deities ; and his Jewish compatriots would also know of whom he spoke, for they were familiar with the expression, " The Word of the Lord came."

A Proper Noun. Always spell " Word " with a capital W.

The Invisible Revealed. As thoughts are invisible, so is God ; as thoughts to become known, must be embodied in words, so God, to make Himself known to mankind revealed Himself in Christ.

No Beginning. The Word was prior to all created things, therefore the Lord Jesus is no part of creation. He did not begin to exist when the Heavens and the earth were made ; the Word had *no* beginning.

A Separate Person. The Word and God are not synonymous terms The Word is not itself God. The Word is distinct from the Father (" with God "), therefore is a separate Person. Yet the Word is one with the Father, one in nature (not inferior—" was God "), and one in affection (note the force of " with," *i.e.,* " leaning upon ").

A Great Painter's god. The last words of Turner, the great landscape painter, who revelled in the wonderful effects produced by light, were, " The sun is God." How could a world create itself ?

Working Together. God the Father created nothing without God the Son (verse 3). How slow we are to learn that we are nothing, and " without Christ we can do nothing " (John 15. 5).

All Existence. Through Him all existence came into being" (verse 3, M.).

THE LIFE AND THE LIGHT

I. JESUS, THE LIFE OF MEN

1. The **Reservoir** of Life, ... verse 4
2. The **Ministry** of Life,.. .. .. .. ,, 4

II. JESUS, THE LIGHT OF MEN

1. The **Ministry** of Light .. .. .. ,, 5
2. The **Triumph** of Light .. .. .. ,, 5
3. The **Witness** of the Light .. .. .. verses 6-8
4. The **Identity** of the Light .. .. .. verse 9
5. The **Mission** of the Light, ... ,, 9

Fundamental Needs. Life and light are two of the elementary and fundamental needs of mankind.

Key-words. Life and Light are two of the key-words of John's writings.

The Physical Order. Observe, life first, then light (verse 4). We need life first in order to enjoy light. All the light in the world is of no use to a dead man.

The Spiritual Order. Spiritually the order is reversed, for we need light before life, though light is never enjoyed until life has been received.

The Great Dynamo. The Lord Jesus is the reservoir of both physical and spiritual life. He is the great Dynamo of the Universe.

The Ministry of Life. In the irrational creatures life is manifested in mere activity of muscle ; in man it appears as " light," intellectual and moral light, the light of reason and conscience.

Shining in Darkness. The Lord as light shone in primeval darkness, and His life on earth was a shining in moral and spiritual darkness.

The Light Triumphant. How triumphant was that light, " the darkness did not master it " (M.), " Overcome it " (R.V.) (verse 5).

John Baptist. John Baptist, referred to by Christ as a " light " (John 5. 35. A different Greek word is here used to that in John 1. 4, and means only a " candle "), was " sent " (verse 6), and " came " (verse 7) as a witness to the Light.

A Common Name. You may have a common name, like John had, and yet not be a common man.

An Inward Light. Some think that the ministry of the light (verse 9) means that Christ lighteth every man and woman on earth with an inward light of grace, sufficient to save if only used.

Moffatt's Rendering. Moffatt's rendering, however, seems to be the true meaning : " The real Light, which enlightens every man, was coming then into the world."

All Mankind Benefited. The Lord Jesus shines for the common benefit of all mankind. Like the sun in the heavens, He is free to all.

RECEIVING CHRIST

I. ITS HISTORY

1. **The Three Steps.** (a) Comprehended not ..   verse   5
                    (b) Knew Him not,   ..   ,,   10
                    (c) Received Him not ..   ,,   11

2. **Christ not Received.** Being misunderstood
and unrecognised, He was not received..   vv. 10, 11

3. **Before Incarnation.** " He was in the world "
(Prior to Incarnation) ..   ..   ..   verse 10

4. **The Incarnation.** " He came unto His
own " (the Incarnation), ...   ,,   11

5. **Received in Heaven.** Praise God for Acts
3. 21. Though rejected here, He was
received up in Glory, and the time is near
when He will be received down here.

II. ITS IMPORTANCE

1. **Salvation Depends on It.** From the human
side of salvation everything depends
upon " receiving." What it means to us
is seen in Col. 2. 6, 7.

2. **Necessary for New Birth.** There can be no
new birth without receiving Christ   ..   ,,   12

III. ITS SIGNIFICANCE

" **Receive** "—not merely admire. Receive
     " **Him**," and not a mere creed ..   ..   ,,   12

IV. ITS REASONABLENESS

When God makes our regeneration and salvation dependent upon this definite act He is only asking us to
do with His greatest Gift what we have already done
with His lesser gifts of coal, iron, gold, pearls, etc.

V. ITS RESULTS

1. Willingness to Forsake Sin   ..   ..   Heb. 11. 17
2. Adoption and New Birth, ...   Gal. 4. 5
3. Difficult Tasks become Easy, ...   John 6. 21
4. Power to Perceive Spiritual Things   ..   Mark 10. 51
5. Ever Present Help in Trouble ..   ..   Luke 10. 38
6. Be Received by Him in Heaven..   ..   John 14. 3

A Change of Interests. Just as Abraham, because he had received the
promises, was willing to part with his darling son, so when we receive
Christ we find we have no more use for those things that were everything
to us before. Other blessings follow.

REALITY

One Translation of the New Testament here uses the
word " Reality " instead of " Truth "

I. THE GOD OF REALITY
Our blessed Lord was full of reality as well as
of graciousness   ..   ..   verse 14
1. **Full.** Not a scanty measure.
2. **Full of Grace.** Graciousness, winsomeness.
3. **Real Grace.** In Christ there is reality as
well as graciousness.

II. THE SPIRIT OF REALITY
The Holy Spirit is the Spirit of Reality   John 14. 17

III. A BOOK OF REALITY
The Bible is a Book of Reality,   ..   John 17. 17

IV. A WORSHIP OF REALITY
God demands a worship that is real .. John 4. 23, 24

V. A LIFE OF REALITY
Grace and reality are ours through Jesus Christ.
We can only become real Christians and
live real lives through Him   ..   ..   verse 17

Reality for Truth. My attention was arrested a while ago by noting the use of the word " Reality " for " Truth." Reality is " what is real."

Reality or Pretence. In Christ there is reality as well as graciousness. It is possible for reality and graciousness to be divorced, to have no reality in our graciousness; that is to say, our graciousness to be only conventional, only a veneer, a pretence. Our Lord was full of reality.

The Spirit of Reality. The Holy Spirit is the Spirit of Reality. There are lying spirits abroad; He is the Spirit of Truth, the Spirit that hates unreality.

Shadow and Substance. The Law was but the shadow of good things to come; the Lord Jesus brought the substance, the glorious reality.

Reality in Worship. God and Christ expect reality in our worship—a drawing nigh to Him in heart as well as in speech; not only repeating nice words, the language of the lips, but words that are also the language of the heart.

Reality in Daily Life. We desire, and indeed demand " reality " in food, clothing, patriotism, etc. If goods are sold as " *all* wool " we expect " all wool," reality.

Reality in Christians. The world expects and demands reality in Christians.

SECTION **1**

LIFE OFFERED

JOHN 1:19—12:50

CHRIST OFFERING HIMSELF TO THE WORLD
AS LIFE

JOHN THE BAPTIST'S WITNESS

John the Baptist bare witness of the Lord, and declared
Him to be—

I. THE SUPERIOR ONE .. .. .. vv. 15, 27
John declared Christ's dignity and rank to be
above and beyond his own.

II. THE PRE-EXISTENT ONE .. .. .. verse 15
John declared Jesus was his senior, though he
was, according to the flesh, six months
older than Jesus. Ah, Jesus is the Eternal
Son of God !

III. THE PERFECT ONE .. .. ,, 16
Jesus was perfect, for " fulness " dwelt in Him.
Every trait in His character was evenly
balanced.

IV. THE BOUNTIFUL ONE ,, 16
In Him dwelt "fulness" that we might
possess it and supply our spiritual wants.

V. THE GREATER ONE .. .. ,, 17
John declares Jesus Christ as greater than
Moses, the great Law-giver.

VI. THE REVEALING ONE .. .. .. ,, 18
John describes Jesus as the great Revealer
of God.

VII. THE BELOVED ONE .. .. .. ,, 18
John does not speak of Jesus as the son of
Mary or Joseph, but as the " Only Begotten
Son of the Father."

The Apostle's Notice of the Prophet. Unlike the other Gospel writers,
John glances very slightly at the Baptist's appearance, habits, and style
of preaching, but dwells with emphasis on the testimony which the prophet bore to the Messiahship of Jesus.

Important to the Jews. To the Jews of that day John's witness was of
the utmost importance.

The Baptist's Humility. John seemed unwilling to speak of himself,
and only did so in answer to urgent inquiries.

Coming Events. The coming of the solitary and suffering Christ was
foreshadowed by the appearing of the solitary and suffering Baptist.

The Inferior One. The Rabbis said : " Every office which a servant
will do for his master, a scholar should perform for his teacher, except
loosing his sandal-thong." Yet this exceptionally menial office the Baptist
declared HE was not worthy of performing for Jesus.

In the Bosom. " Which is IN (not has come out of) the bosom of the
Father " (verse 18). He yet remained in the bosom of the Father when
He became infant on earth.

JOHN THE BAPTIST'S GOSPEL

The Lord Jesus in Three Offices

I. THE SIN BEARER .. .. verse 29
1. **Saviour**—" Lamb."
2. **Very Great Saviour**—" Lamb of God " (a Hebrewism denoting something very great).
3. **Complete Saviour**—" taketh away."
4. **Almighty Saviour**—" sin of the world."
5. **Perpetual Saviour**—" taketh." Note the present tense. That He daily takes it away is the experience of repentant souls. Surely this phrase declares the perpetual efficacy of Christ's death.

II. THE LIFE GIVER .. .. ,, 33
The Lord is declared to be the Source of Spiritual Life and Power through the baptism **with** and **in** the Spirit.

III. THE IDEAL .. .. ,, 36
The Lord is here placed before us as the Ideal. Oh, to be as meek, gentle, pure, and patient as lambs, especially the Lamb of God.

The Baptist's Welcome. Our Lord, on returning from His temptation in the wilderness, came straight to John, to be welcomed with these wondrous and rapturous words.

A Triple Testimony. The testimony of the Baptist was 1. Repent! (Matt. 3. 2) ; 2. Behold! (John 1. 29) ; 3. Believe! (John 3. 36).

A Lamb. At the Passover it was " a lamb for an house " (Exod. 12. 3). At Calvary it was " a Lamb for a world " (verse 29).

The Lamb Provided. *The Question*—Where is the Lamb ? (Gen. 22. 7). *The Promise*—God will provide a Lamb (Gen. 22. 8). *The Answer*—Behold the Lamb of God (John 1. 29).

Three Beholds. 1. Behold the Lamb ! (verse 29) ; 2. Behold the Man ! (John 19. 5) ; 3. Behold the Lion ! (Rev. 5. 5).

A Word in Season. 1. The Baptist's subject was *Christ.* 2. His manner was *earnest.* 3. His message was *practical.* 4. His time was *short.* His appeal was *powerful.* His word was *fruitful.*

Note the Order. Before we are asked to make Him our Ideal, we are pressed to accept Him as Sin-Bearer and Life-Giver. No one can do as Jesus did unless the burden of guilt has been removed, and unless they are indwelt by God the Holy Spirit.

JOHN THE BAPTIST'S DISCOVERY

How John the Baptist discovered his Cousin according
to the Flesh to be the Divine One

I. A STARTLING STATEMENT .. .. verse 26

The Messiah was already in their midst ! How
John's challenging answer must have
startled them.

II. A FRANK CONFESSION .. .. .. ,, 31

John and the Lord Jesus were cousins, therefore verse 31 means that he knew Him as
his relative but not as his Messiah. He
certainly knew Him as One so good that
he felt unworthy to baptise Him (Matt.
3. 14), a very notable and manly confession
as to the influence and character of Christ's
life prior to His baptism.

III. A TIMELY EXPLANATION .. .. .. ,, 31

John, at the approach of Jesus, explains to
his hearers the reason of his mission.

IV. A VALUABLE DISCOVERY .. .. .. vv. 32-34

It was by the outpouring of the Spirit that
John became aware of the Messiahship
of Jesus.

Introducing the Lord. Christian workers must see to it that they not
only give information about the Lord, but seek to introduce their hearers
to Him. This John did.

John a Sent One. " He that sent me " (verse 33). Then John was a
sent one.

Familiarity with God. " The same said unto me "—holy, reverent,
familiarity with God. Only they who know their God, and live in communion with Him, are fit to proclaim the Lord Jesus.

The Sacred Symbol. " Upon Him " (verse 32). As a crown gently
placed upon the head of a King, at once an ornament and a badge of
sovereignty, so this sacred symbol pointed out the Son and Heir to the
Throne of the Universe.

A Distant Relationship. It is possible to be related to Jesus by the ties
of faith and yet know little of Him.

Deeper Knowledge. By being filled with the Spirit we get that deeper
knowledge.

DISCIPLESHIP

I. ITS GENESIS

1. A Preacher's Clear **Testimony** .. .. verse 36
2. A Brother's Loving **Witness** .. .. ,, 41

II. ITS DEVELOPMENT

1. Encouraging **Recognition** (Jesus turned) .. ,, 38
2. A Searching **Question** (What seek ye ?) .. ,, 38
3. An Imperative **Command** (Come and see !) ,, 39
4. First Hand **Knowledge** (They came and saw) ., 39

III. ITS PROGRESS

1. **Salvation** (They followed Jesus) .. .. ,, 37
2. **Friendship** (They came with Him) .. ,, 39
3. **Communion** (They abode with Him) .. ,, 39
4. **Service** (He brought him to Jesus) .• ,, 42

The First Disciples. This study is important for many reasons. For one thing, here we have the securing of the first two disciples, the beginning of that marvellous stream of converts which has never run dry.

The Result of Testifying. These first two disciples were gained by John the Baptist's clear testimony concerning the Lord. We may not be very clever, yet we can be clear and so point sinners to Christ.

A Brother's Witness. A brother's loving witness also had to do with the source of this wonderful stream of discipleship. " First " (verse 41)—my first duty. " Findeth "—put himself about. " We," not I—his humility. See John 15. 8.

Encouraging Recognition. That early discipleship was developed by our Lord's encouraging recognition (" turned," verse 38), searching question, compelling thought, and by His imperative " Now " (verse 39). Evidently they thought only of securing His address that day, and calling to see Him another day. He bade them come *that day*. Well was it that they followed then, for He left that part of the country the next day.

What Seek Ye ? Jesus will test the motives of those who would follow Him.

Progress in Discipleship. Discipleship begins by beholding Him as Lamb of God ; and it progresses as we enter into friendship and communion with Him, and enter into His service.

Look Translated Gazed. " He *gazed* at Jesus " (verse 36, M.). " Jesus gazed at him " (verse 42, M.). A gaze, not a mere glance.

THE CALLING OF PETER

Peter is found by Andrew, his brother, who brings him to Christ.
Christ changes the name of His new follower from Simon to Peter

I. THOU ART

A Sad Reminder. Weak, vacillating, impulsive, and all that the word " Simon " is synonymous of.

II. THOU SHALT BE

A Glorious Prophecy. As firm as a rock, and all that " Peter " stands for. This was fulfilled at Pentecost.

Quiet Andrew did a great work when he brought the boisterous Peter to Christ.

An Early Search. For " *He first* findeth," M. renders " In the *morning.*"

A Penetrating Look. For "When Jesus *beheld* him," M. gives " Jesus *gazed* at him," significant of the intensity and penetration of our Lord's look.

An Important Event. When one remembers the position Peter occupied in the early Christian Church, one notes the importance of our Lord's first interview with him.

The Past—the Future. The Lord reminded Peter what he was, and then what he not only might, but should become by infinite grace.

Saving and Sanctifying Grace. The Lord alone can reveal to us our true self. Only by His grace can we discover our own sinful state. But He also points out the glorious possibility of becoming by His grace all that He desires us to be.

Taking the Initiative. How easy it is to follow Jesus in a crowd, but in every company or family there is need for one with courage enough to step out for Christ, and be an example to others.

The Evidence of Faith. Peter's faith was evidenced by his *following* Christ. He had no time to delay in his decision, for Jesus " walked " and would soon be out of sight (verses 36, 37).

Companying with Christ. That quiet time of close fellowship that Andrew had with Jesus (verse 39) resulted in immediate fruit-bearing. Companying with Christ leads to clearness of views and boldness of action. He had sought and found the Messias—his testimony was clear and persuasive. Can we be truly following Christ if our lives are not constraining others to follow Him?

THE CALL OF NATHANIEL

I. PHILIP'S WAY WITH NATHANIEL

II. CHRIST'S WAY WITH NATHANIEL

A Day of Finding. This was indeed *a blessed day of finding.* Note the diversity of the ways we are led to the Lord : Jesus found Philip ; Philip found Nathaniel ; John and Andrew found the Lord through John the Baptist ; Andrew found Peter.

Hot Haste Searching. Philip, when found, lost no time in seeking others, but went in hot haste after his friend Nathaniel.

A Bold Reception. What a rude shock this new convert received ! Nathaniel's treatment of the good news was like a cold water douche.

Bring Men to Christ. But Philip neither argued with Nathaniel nor ignored his difficulties ; he instinctively knew how useless it was to reason with men about Christ's claims so long as they were not in His presence. One look, one word from Himself, will go further to persuade a man than all that anyone can say. Philip's Gospel was not "it" but "Him." He met the "How ?" of the inquirer with the "Come !" of the Gospel.

Christ's Way. Notice the Lord's treatment of Nathaniel :

1. "No *guile.*" He does not say, "*No guilt.*" The mark is not sinlessness, but sincerity.

2. Nathaniel's astonished question (v. 48). The eye of Jesus had penetrated the leafy veil of the dense foliage of the fig trees. He is a witness to our prayers and vows.

3. Like a wise teacher, who lets his pupils at the very beginning get a glimpse of how much lies ahead for them to learn, so the Lord gives Nathaniel a hint as to the great tract of yet uncomprehended knowledge of Him which lies before them.

4. "Angels *ascending* and descending," not descending and ascending— at present earth is their home. R. renders this "Angels of God ascending and descending *unto* the Son of Man."

Nazareth. Where Jesus was brought up. An insignificant, perhaps an infamous town. But Jesus came "out of Heaven," not "out of Nazareth."

THE MARRIAGE IN CANA

Golden Lessons from this, our Lord's first Sign

I. SACRED JOYS HALLOWED
Christ hallows the sweet, sacred joys of marriage and of family life.

II. EARTHLY JOYS SANCTIFIED
Christ sanctified and elevated all earthly joys. This incident proclaims the sanctity of marriage.

III. EMBARRASSMENT RELIEVED
Christ gives speedy relief to His embarrassed friends.

IV. PRAYERFUL HABITS UTILISED
Mary had been accustomed to lean on Jesus, and turn to Him in her difficulties. How this habit helped her in this unexpected crisis.

V. CHRIST'S GREATNESS EXHIBITED
Christ's greatness was quietly yet unmistakably exhibited in this display of His easy mastery of nature.

VI. MARY'S FAITH DECLARED
The Gospel of the blessed Virgin is declared in her striking statement of faith in Christ.

VII. BEST BLESSINGS DEFERRED
The Lord keeps His BEST till the last.

The First Miracle. This was the Lord's first public appearance, and the very first miracle He ever performed (verse 11). The glory of Christ did not begin here; it was only manifested (verse 11). For "glory" we could read "greatness." Moses' first miracle was turning water into blood (death). Christ's was turning water into wine (life).

"**Mother.**" In this Gospel Mary is called "Mother," never "Mary."

"**And His Disciples.**" "Jesus was called *and His disciples*." If we lose friends by following Christ we gain others.

"**Woman.**" "Woman" (verse 4) had not then the meaning it would have with us. It was the ordinary Greek term of address to all classes of females. It is used here with the utmost reverence and affection.

Mary Rebuked. Roman Catholics attempt to draw from this incident encouragement in favour of the Virgin Mary's intercession in Heaven for sinners. This petition, the only one we ever find addressed to our Lord by the Virgin Mary, brought from Him an immediate rebuke.

Helpful Habits. Mary had ever been accustomed to lean on Him, and turn to Him in her difficulties. What a blessed example for us to copy. Habits thus formed help us in unexpected difficulties.

Bengel's Opinion. Bengel thought verse 3 was meant by her as a gentle hint for Him and His disciples to depart. Calvin thought it was a hint for Jesus to occupy the minds of the guests by a profitable discourse, so that they would not notice the deficiency. It is simpler to view this as the result of Mary's invariable habit of turning to Him in her difficulties.

The Water Blushed. Milton wrote: "The conscious water saw its Lord and blushed."

CLEANSING THE TEMPLE

I. THE NARRATIVE

    1. He went down—geographically correct   ..   verse 12
    2. The Jews' Passover ..   ..   ,,   13
    3. The Lord's first public act.
    4. The first of the two cleansings.
    5. Christ acted before He spake.
    6. His work began at the House of God.

II. THE LESSONS

    1. The Lord's **Zeal** for the Sanctuary.
    2. The Lord's **Care** for the Proselytes.
    3. The Lord's **Ideal** for His People.
    4. The Lord's **Scourge** for Evil Habits.

The Jews' Passover. One of the peculiarities of John's Gospel is the occurrence of the word " Jew." This word is only found *once* in Matthew ; *twice* in Mark ; *twice* in Luke ; but appears over *sixty* times in John.

The Two Cleansings. There were two cleansings of the Temple. John alone records this. That recorded in the other Gospels (Matt. 21. 12 ; Mark 11. 15 ; Luke 19. 45) was the second cleansing.

Began and Ended. Our Lord began and ended His public ministry by cleansing the Temple.

Prophecy Fulfilled. Was this not a fulfilment of Malachi 3. 1 ?

Actions Before Words. Christ acted before He spoke. " Began both *to do* and *teach* " (Acts 1. 1).

Began at God's House. Why did our Lord begin His work at the House of God ?

1. Because He knew the Temple was the real heart of the nation. Belief in God was their strength and hope.

2. For the sake of the Gentiles. Gentile converts to Judaism were not allowed to pass beyond the outer court. It was here this market was held. How could the Gentiles worship amidst all the din and confusion of a market ?

The Lord's Zeal. The Lord was very zealous for the purity of—

1. The Earthly Sanctuary—the Temple of His own Father (verse 16).

2. The Human Sanctuary—the Temple of His own Body (verse 21).

The Lord's Care. Note the Lord's anxious care for the Gentile proselytes mentioned above.

The Lord's Ideal. That we, His human temples, be homes of prayer.

The Lord's Scourge. There is no one like the Lord to drive out of our lives the evil therein.

My Father's House is not to be turned into a shop (M., verse 16).

The Sinner's Scourge. Sinners prepare and provide their own scourges. The scourge was made from material the guilty ones had secured their cattle with. Sins and evil habits will prove a scourge by which the sinner will be whipped.

THE NEW BIRTH

The subject which formed the marvellous conversation between Jesus and Nicodemus, the Jewish Ruler

I. ITS NECESSITY
The natural man is impotent to see or enter
the Kingdom   ..   ..   verse 3

II. ITS SUBJECTS
1. For "**a man**" (verse 3), that is, anyone and every one.
2. For "**ye**" (verse 7), the Nicodemuses, who are sinners though moral, upright, who require no reformation.

III. ITS NATURE
A change **of** nature, not a change **in** nature.

IV. ITS MODE

1. **Author,**	.. God,	..	.. 1 Peter 1. 3
2. **Channel,**	.. Christ,	..	.. John 1. 11, 12
3. **Executive,**	.. Spirit,	..	.. John 3. 6-8
4. **Medium,**	.. Word,	..	.. 1 Peter 1. 2, 3
			James 1. 18

V. ITS PROOF
The recipient becomes a partaker of the life of Christ Himself. See John's First Epistle 5. 1 ; 2. 29 ; 3. 9 ; 5. 18 ; 4. 7 ; 5. 4 ; 5. 18.

Life Lost and Regained. In Genesis 3 we learn how life was lost, in John 3 how life is regained.

Distinguish, but Don't Separate. You may distinguish between conversion and regeneration, but you cannot separate them.

Regeneration. "The necessity of the new birth grows out of the incapacity of the natural man to 'see' or 'enter into' the kingdom of God. However gifted, moral, or refined, the natural man is absolutely blind to spiritual truth, and impotent to enter the kingdom ; for he can neither obey, understand, nor please God " (S.B.).

The Great Change. Regeneration is not a change *in* nature, but a change *of* nature. The old nature remains unchanged, but by regeneration another nature is imparted. It is not a reformation of the old nature, but a creative act of the Holy Spirit.

Water and Spirit. John 3. 5 has puzzled many.

1. Cranmer in 1553 wrote : "All that be washed with water be not washed with the Holy Spirit."

2. "Except a man be born of water *Kai* (Greek) Spirit." The lexicographers tell us that the conjunction *Kai* may have an epexegetical meaning, and may be (as it frequently is) used to amplify what has gone before ; that it may have the sense of "even," or "namely." And thus the reading is, "Except a man be born of water, even spirit, or spiritual water."

3. John Calvin, a learned Greek scholar, rendered it : "Except a man be born of water, even of the Spirit."

4. "Water—spirit "—"Not two things, but one, by which the latter noun becomes a superlative and emphatic adjective, determining the meaning and nature of the former noun " (Bullinger).

THE WIND—AN EMBLEM

The wind is used as a Favourite Emblem of the Holy Spirit, and suggests His active and powerful Operations

I. THE NEW BIRTH

1. **A Sovereign Work.** "The Spirit bloweth where it listeth" (R.V.) ..   ..   ..   verse 8
2. **A Secret Work.** "Thou knowest not whence it cometh" (R.V.) ..   ..   ,, 8
3. **A Self-Evidencing Work.** "Thou hearest the voice thereof" (R.V.) ..   ..   ..   ,, 8

II. THE WIND

1. **Invisible in its Essence.** A vital unseen force, but a very real one.
2. **Mysterious in its Action.** An undefinable force, known by its mighty effects.
3. **Sovereign in its Operation.** Utterly beyond all human control or human laws.
4. **Irresistible in its Movement.** What could withstand the *full* might of such a force.
5. **Searching in its Work.** Winnows away the chaff. Demolishes all that is unsound or insecure.
6. **Cleansing in its Service.** A mighty cleansing agent, purifying the foul.
7. **Varied in its Direction.** Comes from four quarters.
   (*a*) The **East** Wind of foul weather—Judgment
   (*b*) The **West** Wind of moist weather—Refreshment
   (*c*) The **North** Wind of fair weather—Encouragement
   (*d*) The **South** Wind of warm weather—Enjoyment

Occasion. Perhaps a gust of wind swept round the chamber where Nicodemus sat listening to Jesus, and gave occasion for this condensed parable.

Nature Personified. The Bible often personifies nature. The Lord spoke of "stones crying out." The word for Wind, Breath, and Spirit in Hebrew and Greek is the same.

The Spirit Unseen. The Holy Spirit cannot be diagnosed or seen. He is none the less real.

The Spirit's Sovereignty. The Holy Spirit acts in the sovereignty of His grace.

Irresistible and Everywhere. The wind is irresistible, the Spirit is omnipotent. The wind is everywhere, the Spirit is omnipresent.

The Spirit's Activities. He is the Begetter of the new life. He is the Purifier of the heart. He is the Opposer of the flesh. He is the Sanctifier of the saint. He is the Producer of the fruits of righteousness.

THE BRAZEN SERPENT

And a Study of Christ's "Musts"

I. THE EMBLEM

1. Christ's View of Humanity.

a. *Poisoned by Sin*, like the bite of a venemous serpent, which is—
  (1) Diffused in its action.
  (2) Rapid in its progress.
  (3) Painful in its operation.
  (4) Deadly in its result.

b. *Miserable* on this account.

c. *Restless*, like a fever-tossed patient.

d. *Hopeless*, for the Israelites had no cure in the desert ; and earth has no cure for the sting of sin.

2. Christ's View of Himself.

a. *Only Means of Healing and Life* to a sin-poisoned world.

b. *The Remedy Lies in His Death.*

c. *Which would be Conspicuous.* "Lifted up."

d. *Accessible to All.* "Whosoever."

e. *Life-giving*, for " in Him " (R.V.) is the great reservoir of life.

3. Christ's View of Faith.

II. THE PRINCIPLE

" Must " is a hard word, describing a great necessity. Christ speaks of that which dominated His life and shaped even small actions, for the word is often found in connection with His life and work.

1. His Father's Business,	..	..	Luke 2. 49
2. Soul-Seeking,	..	..	..	John 4. 4
3. His Work,	..	..	..	John 9. 4
4. Ingathering,	..	..	..	John 10. 16
5. The Cross,	..	..	..	John 3. 14
6. The Indwelling,	..	..	Luke 19. 5

Justification. Our Lord had been giving Nicodemus a lesson on Regeneration, now He gives a lesson on Justification. Here we have the second of the instances in this Gospel in which the Lord uses an illustration from the Old Testament.

THE GOSPEL PEARL

Love in its Four Dimensions (Eph. 3. 18)

An Outline by Prof. CLOW

I. ITS BREADTH

" For God so loved the WORLD."

II. ITS LENGTH

" That He gave HIS ONLY BEGOTTEN SON."
The test of love is to what length it will go.

III. ITS DEPTH

" That WHOSOEVER BELIEVETH in Him should not perish."

IV. ITS HEIGHT

" But have EVERLASTING LIFE."

Luther says : " These words are the Bible in miniature."

Love and Salvation. " Love is the one ground of the Divine purpose, and salvation the one aim."

The Missionary Nott announced this text to Tahitians. They asked : " Is this really true ? " He repeatedly affirmed it. " Oh ! " they exclaimed, " and canst thou speak of such love without tears ? "

" **The Love . . . which Passeth Knowledge.**" What is this but a sublime attempt to indicate how immeasurable love is ?

" **The Test of Love** is to what length it will go. Love is not love which will not die, or make those sacrifices often more bitter and cruel than death."

Original. John 3. 16 is one of the great original utterances of Scripture. It is difficult for us to imagine how startling this statement must have been to Nicodemus. Before the Lord Jesus came into this world no one ever dreamt of saying that God loves the *world*. Nicodemus knew that God loved *Israel*, but never dreamt He also loved the Gentiles. On this verse Calvin said : " Christ brought life, because the Heavenly Father loves the human race, and wishes that they should not perish."

" **So Loved.**" Indefinite past tense, denoting the universal eternal existence of this love.

GOD'S GIFT

When put in the form of a Questionaire, this text makes a simple yet effective Outline

I. WHO IS THE GIVER ?   ..   ..   ..   GOD
   1. His Person.
   2. His Work.
   3. His Power.

II. WHO IS THE GIFT ?   ..   ..   ..   JESUS
   1. The Son of God.
   2. His Coming by Incarnation.
   3. His Life and Death.

III. HOW IS IT GIVEN ?   ..   ..   ..   IN LOVE
   1. Magnitude of that Love.
   2. In Spite of the World's Hatred.

IV. TO WHOM IS IT GIVEN ?   ..   ..   THE WORLD
   1. **Universally.** None excluded.
   2. **Individually.** To each one separately.

V. WHY IS IT GIVEN ?   ..   SHOULD NOT PERISH
   1. The Danger Man is in.
   2. The Desire of his Creator.

VI. HOW IT IS ACCEPTED ?   WHOSOEVER BELIEVETH
   1. **Personally.** There must be individual acceptance
   2. **Simplicity.** He that believeth—HATH

Becon's Outline. This was an outline given by Becon, Chaplain to Archbishop Cranmer.

Greatness of the Gift. The depth and intensity of God's love can only be measured by the unworthiness of the object, and the greatness of the Gift.

Gave His Son. This was love's great sacrifice to win back an alien world from the love of sin, and the power of the enemy.

Value of the Gift. God's appointed Lamb alone could suffice to meet the world's dire need.

Home of Incurables. This world is a vast hospital full of incurables dying from the ravages of sin, and without care apart from the Divine remedy.

The Two Sides. Loving and giving are God's side. Believing and having are man's side.

LOVE

In this verse we have the Copestone of all the Thoughts of Love. Here is to be found Love in its—

I. LOFTIEST SOURCE	God
II. MIGHTIEST FORCE	so
III. PUREST FORM	loved
IV. LARGEST SCALE	the world
V. GREATEST MANIFESTATION	that He gave
VI. COSTLIEST GIFT	His only begotten Son
VII. WIDEST SCOPE	that whosoever
VIII. SIMPLEST TERMS	believeth
IX. SWEETEST THEME	in Him
X. STRONGEST POWER	should not perish
XI. SUREST PLEDGE	but have
XII. NOBLEST ORDER	everlasting
XIII. RICHEST POSSESSION	life
XIV. HIGHEST PURPOSE	The whole verse

Die. " Love is not love which will not die, or make the sacrifices often more bitter and cruel than death."

Eternity. John 3. 16 is a word that whispers and sighs, and soliloquises through the eternities. And no fitting word can be found to describe love—for it is unspeakable.

GOD'S GREAT LOVE

The Greatness of the Love of God as Exhibited in this exhaustless Verse.   It is Great—

I. IN ITS OBJECT
1. The World in all its **Darkness.**
2. The World in all its **Guilt.**
3. The World in all its **Hopelessness.**

II. IN ITS PLAN
1. To make **Known** His Salvation to every **Creature.**
2. To make **Possible** His Salvation to every **Sinner.**
3. To make **Certain** His Salvation to every **Believer.**

III. IN ITS AGENT
1. No one **Higher** could be **Found.**
2. No one **Lower** would be **Sufficient.**

IV. IN ITS MANIFESTATION
1. He Calculated the World's Need.
2. He Spared Not His Own Son.

V. IN ITS RESULTS
1. The **Knowledge** of the **Pardon** of God.
2. The **Enjoyment** of the **Presence** of God.
3. The **Worship** of the **Person** of God.

VI. IN ITS CONDITIONS
1. Whosoever **Believeth** hath Everlasting Life.
2. Whosoever **Cometh** is not cast out.
3. Whosoever **Confesseth** is born of God (1 John 4. 15).

VII. IN ITS DISINTERESTEDNESS
1. People of every **Age.**
2. People of every **Race.**
3. People of every **Class.**

Its Plan. Embracing and harmonising such opposing interests as God and the world; His Justice and His Love; the debt of man and his inability to discharge it.

TWELVE GREATEST THINGS

I. THE GREATEST LOVER	.. .. ..	God
II. THE GREATEST DEGREE	.. .. ..	so loved
III. THE GREATEST COMPANY	.. ..	the world
IV. THE GREATEST ACT	.. ..	that He gave
V. THE GREATEST GIFT	..	His only begotten Son
VI. THE GREATEST OPPORTUNITY	..	that whosoever
VII. THE GREATEST SIMPLICITY	..	believeth
VIII. THE GREATEST ATTRACTION	.. ..	in Him
IX. THE GREATEST PROMISE	.. ..	should not perish
X. THE GREATEST DIFFERENCE	.. .. ..	but
XI. THE GREATEST CERTAINTY	.. ..	have
XII. THE GREATEST POSSESSION	..	everlasting life

Amazing Depth. There is an amazing and bewildering depth of truth here. " Perhaps no verse in the Bible has been so much explained as this ; perhaps no verse can be so little explained. Most young preachers have sermons upon it ; older men learn that its meaning must be felt and thought rather than spoken."—*Canon Watkins.*

Ground and Aim. Love is the one ground of the Divine purpose, and Salvation the one aim.

The World. It is well for us to remember that all through the New Testament " the world " does not only mean men, but *sinful* men, men away from God. Every sinful soul on the earth has God's love resting upon him, and stretching forth its hands to him.

GOD'S GREAT LOVE

AND WHAT IT IS

An Outline by Dr. F. E. MARSH

I. EXPRESSIVE IN ITS ACTION
" For God so loved "

II. EXTRAORDINARY IN ITS CHOICE
" the world "

III. EXPENSIVE IN ITS SACRIFICE
" that He gave His only begotten Son,"

IV. EXTENSIVE IN ITS OFFER.
" that whosoever "

V. EXCLUSIVE IN ITS BESTOWMENT
" believeth in Him "

VI. EXCEPTIONAL IN ITS WORK
" should not perish "

VII. ETERNAL IN ITS BLESSEDNESS
" but have everlasting life."

Why We Love Him. A little girl was playing with her doll in a room where her mother was busily engaged in some literary work. When she had finished her task she turned to the wee girlie, saying : " You can come now, Alice ! " The child ran to her, exclaiming : " I am *so* glad, for I wanted to love you so much." " But I thought you were very happy with dolly ! " was the lady's reply. " Yes, mother, I was, but I soon get tired of loving her, for *she cannot love me back*." " And is that why you love me, because I love you back ? " " That is one ' why,' " replied the wee philosopher, " but not the first or best one. You loved me *when I was too little to love you back*." Observe some reasons for loving Him : (1) He first loved (1 John 4. 19). (2) He hears my prayer (Psa. 116. 1). (3) He cares for me, preserves, and rewards (Psa. 31. 23). (4) He is with us, and one with us (1 Sam. 18. 16). (5) He overrules all for our good (Rom. 8. 28). (6) He gives amazingly generously (1 Cor. 2. 9).

THE LAKE AND THE RIVER

An Outline by Dr. ALEXANDER MACLAREN, commended and quoted by Sir W. ROBERTSON NICOLL in his " Lamp of Sacrifice "

I. THE LAKE

" God so loved the world."

1. **How Wide the Lake.** " The world."

2. **He Loves All** because He Loves **Each.**

" Not as I love India."

3. **Some never See this Lake.**

So absorbed are they in the things of time and sense.

II. THE RIVER

" That He gave His only begotten Son."

1. **Its Source.** The Lake makes a River for itself. " He gave."

2. **Its Course.** " His only Son."

The course of true love never did run smooth.

III. THE PITCHER

" That whosoever believeth in Him."

1. **Necessary.** The river will not quench one's thirst unless he has something with which to lift the water.

2. **Essential.** All this love may flow past in full flood and never reach us, unless we draw and appropriate it.

IV. THE DRAUGHT

" Should not perish but *have* everlasting life."

1. **Immediate.** The thirst is quenched at once.

2. **Eternal.** No need for earthly water afterwards.

John 4. 13, 14.

" **That's Done It.**" Prebendary Webb-Peploe tells of a man in a trench during the Great War, about to die, asking the man next him how he could get to Heaven. " Can't tell you nothing about it," he replied. But a man a little further on heard, and threw across a little Gospel. " Read John 3. 16," he cried, " that'll tell him." And as the dying man heard those glorious words of verse 16, he said with his last breath, " Thank God, that's done it."

CHRIST'S MISSION

I. ITS OBJECT—Not to Condemn　　..　　..　　verse 17

    1. **Wrong Views.** Nicodemus and his fellow-Jews held the view that when Messiah came He would come with power and great glory, to judge all men, according to Psalm 2. 6 to 9 ; Dan. 7. 9 to 22, etc.

    2. **His Own View.** So save, not to condemn.

II. ITS ISSUE—Condemnation　　..　　..　　..　vv. 18, 19

    1. **Defined,** ..　　..　　..　　..　　..　　..　　verse 19

    2. **Pronounced.** Whilst condemnation was not the object of Christ's mission, it was and is its issue in many cases,　　..　　..　　verse 18

    3. **But Not Executed.** And so it is still possible to escape this issue.

III. ITS TRAGEDY—Those who love darkness and hate the light　　..　　..　　..　vv. 20, 21

    1. **Reasons.** Why men reject the Light.

       (*a*) Because there is not light on *all* points. Because men have not as much light as they wish, they reject what light they can have.

       (*b*) Because their deeds are evil, and this is the largest company.

    2. **Results.** Loving the darkness and hating the light

Oh, the tragedy of it ! The sick man thanks the physician for unfolding a disease concealed ; the traveller thanks the stranger for revealing his danger from lurking robbers ; but the sinner strangely hates those friends who would rescue him from the evil which will ruin him for ever.

Jesus and His Negatives. 1. The Lord Jesus was a master in the use of negatives.

2. The negative method is the system of endeavouring to find out what a thing is by first discovering what it is not.

3. This is the best way of dealing with slow and dull scholars.

4. Examples : " I came, not to call the righteous, but," etc. " The Son of Man came not to be ministered unto," " God sent not His Son," etc.

First and Second Advents. He was sent the first time to be the Saviour ; He will come the second time as Judge. His first coming was to *make* satisfaction for sin, His second coming will be to *obtain* satisfaction for sin.

For " **Condemn** " (verse 17), M. gives " pass sentence on " ; R.V., " judge."

" **The world** " (verse 17). Not merely the Jewish people

JOHN'S LAST TESTIMONY

John the Baptist's Last Declaration concerning the Lord Jesus deserves our closest attention

Verses 31-36. Many think these verses were spoken by the Lord Himself. M., by a re-arrangement of these verses, teaches so. More take them to be John the Baptist's own words. Or were they the comment of the writer of the book ?

Good out of Evil. We have here a splendid instance of how admirably God can bring good out of evil, for a carnal and unkind saying of John's disciples (verses 25 and 26) gives occasion to John for an admirable testimony about Christ.

The Events. (a) Left Jerusalem for surrounding country (verse 22).

(b) Lord Jesus baptised, but only by proxy (verse 22 with 4. 2).

(c) Note the rather slighting way John's disciples referred to the Lord Jesus (verse 26). "See how He has repaid you for your kind commendation."

(d) "All" (verse 26). Surely an exaggeration

(e) Verse 27, "Receive." Surely this means that the power of perceiving or apprehending truth comes from above

Humility of John. What a splendid pattern of true and godly humility we have in verses 27 to 30. The greatest saint in the sight of God is the man who is most thoroughly clothed with humility.

Christ and the Spirit. "God gives Him the Spirit in *no sparing* measure " (34 M.).

THE SAMARITAN WOMAN

I. THE CASE

An adultress. Not shameless. Religious formalist. Proud of her descent (verse 12). Frivolous (verse 15). Perplexed.

II. THE METHOD, in the Art of Soul-winning

1. **Went out of his way** (verse 4). Putting himself to some trouble.
2. **Not bound by conventionality.** "Let no man talk with a woman in the street," advised the Rabbis.
3. **Acted Circumspectly.** A *day-time* interview.
4. **Tactful.**
   - (a) Interviewed alone, the twelve sent away.
   - (b) Did not reprove or scold.
   - (c) Asked a favour.
   - (d) Use of homely metaphor for spiritual truth.
   - (e) Then went to the point (verse 16).
   - (f) Refused to be diverted.
   - (g) Emphasized asking and receiving on part of sinner, not giving.

III. THE RESULT

1. **Conversion.**   2. **Absorption** (verse 28).
3. **Missionary Enthusiasm** (vv. 29 and 30).

IV. THE DOCTRINE

1. **Baptism.** Subordinate to doctrine (verse 2).
2. **Our Lord's Humanity** (verse 6). Laboured to point of weariness.
3. **Spirituality of God** (verse 24). Profoundest sentence in human language.
4. **Refreshment in Spiritual Labour.** Hunger and weariness gone, fresh vigour gained. The joy of a successful soul-winner.

Comparison with Nicodemus. This chapter is a fitting complement to the previous one. In our Lord's dealings with Nicodemus we learn that no religious privilege, no religious forms, no religious training, can avail; nothing but a new creature. In His dealings with the Samaritan woman we see that "no condition, however lowly, no ignorance, however dense; no circumstances, however evil; no character, however bad, can shut us out from the great love of God."

The Holy Spirit. In chapter 3 is spoken of as a Quickening Power, whilst in this chapter He is referred to as an Indwelling Presence.

Drinketh (verse 14). Not merely taste.

TWO KINDS OF FAITH

I. HEARSAY FAITH   ..   ..   verse 39

A Faith which Rests on the Testimony of Another, a "Hearsay" Faith. The townsfolk were impressed by the woman's evident sincerity, "and many believed."

II. EXPERIMENTAL FAITH   ..   ..   ..   vv. 41, 42

A Faith which Rests upon Personal Discovery. They went out to meet the Lord Jesus, and to see and hear Him for themselves, and "many more believed" because they had a personal experience of the Lord Jesus Christ.

We must have First Hand Experience, a faith which rests not merely on the testimony of others, but as the result of personal discovery and personal appropriation.

Simple Opening. This wondrous dialogue begins with a cup of water, and ends with the most sublime revelation of the nature of God and His worship.

She was Not Shameless. This is seen in her going for water when she knew other women would not be there. She went at noon, they always go in the evening.

Jesus called "Lord" (verse 1) for first time in this Gospel.

Sychar (verse 5). Place where eleven of Jacob's sons were buried (Act 7. 16).

The Change in the Woman.

1. In her conversation with Jesus by the well, there was opened up to the woman of Samaria, not only the blotted and blurred scroll of her life, but such a vision of purity and truth, and grace, as she had never known.

2. She came to Jacob's well, but she discovered another well.

3. "The flippancy with which at first she answered our Lord was turned to solemnity."

4. "From being a mocker she became a missionary."

Calvin's Comment on verse 42 seems rather harsh. He says they boasted that their faith now rested on a stronger foundation than a woman's tongue. Yet, with the word "tongue" deleted, the remark is true, though crudely expressed. For her testimony was true, and was blest to their conversion.

Development of Faith. We have here a lesson on the true development of faith—first the hearing of the ear, then personal discovery. Note, faith, 1st, In the presence of the Lord; 2nd, In the Word of the Lord (verse 50); 3rd, In the Deity of the Lord (verse 53).

THE NOBLEMAN'S FAITH

The Lord hungered for a real faith, and so dealt with this nobleman in rather a severe fashion to develop his faith

I. FAITH IN HIS PRESENCE   ..   ..   ..   verse 47

The nobleman thought our Lord's presence was essential to the healing of his son.

Did he come to our Lord, not for the Lord's sake, but only for his son's ? Was he drawn by the strong constraint of an outward need, rather than by the desires of the soul ? Yet our Lord did not turn him away.

II. FAITH IN HIS WORD   ..   ..   ..   „ 50

There is a certain amount of severity in our Lord's reply in verse 48, but He desired to teach the nobleman that **His word was as effective and as effectual as His presence.** " He sent His Word and healed them," wrote the Psalmist.

III. FAITH IN HIMSELF   ..   ..   „ 53

This is the highest form of faith and that which our Lord most desires.

The Success which attended our Lord's two days' mission in Samaria was unusual and most encouraging.

" **After two days** " (verse 43), or rather, " *the* two days."

Jesus in Galilee. If a prophet hath no honour in his own country, why should Jesus go to Galilee, His own country ? Was He searching for a quiet place of retirement ?

The Samaritans had believed *without a miracle* ; the Galileans, because of His miracles (verse 45).

A Long Journey. This nobleman had travelled (verses 20 to 25) miles to seek healing for his son. What earnestness ! The rich have afflictions as well as the poor.

Proof of Faith. He " believed the word " (verse 50), and did not hurry back. Though 1 p.m. when he left the Lord, he did not go back that night. He rested in the Lord, and counted the work done.

AFTER THIRTY-EIGHT YEARS

The history of the man who was waiting for something to happen. He was—

I. **INFIRM,** and he knew it   ..   ..   ..   verse 7

II. **LONGING** for healing ..   ..   ,,   7

III. **FRIENDLESS,** and bemoaned it   ..   ..   ,,   7

IV. **HOPELESS,** and despairing   ..   ..   ..   ,,   7

V. **STARTLED,** and roused by a question   ..   ,,   6

VI. **OBEDIENT** to the Lord's command   ..   ,,   9

VII. **HEALED** because of his faith   ..   ..   ,,   9

VIII. **FOUND IN RIGHT PLACE** afterwards   ..   ,,   14

IX. **COMMISSIONED** for his future life ..   ..   ,,   14

Illustration. A mistress inquired of her servant girl, on her return from Church, what the minister had been preaching upon, when she replied, "The *omnipotent* man." She was not far wrong, for this poor man ceased to be *impotent* when he came into vital touch with the omnipotent Saviour.

The Time. This miracle occurred just one year after (chap. 4. 46 to 54), and is recorded primarily because it marks the beginning of the angry unbelief on the part of the Jewish rulers, and because it formed the occasion for the Lord's great utterance about His Sonship.

The Type. This poor man is a type of those who, convinced of sin and their need of Christ, are postponing decision for Christ until something happens—some singular emotion, remarkable impression, or celestial vision. And they wait, and wait, and wait, but all in vain. Something will happen if they will but come to Christ.

Sin and Disease. It is clear by our Lord's warning (verse 14) that this trouble was the fruit of his own sin. It was a sin of the flesh avenged in the flesh.

Renewal of Hope. Without doubt, the long years of fruitless waiting had quenched the lamp of hope, and He asked the question (verse 6) to rekindle hope.

THE SON OF GOD

Our Lord's Claim to Equality with the Father

I. ITS NEGATIVE ASPECT .. .. .. verse 19
1. He had the **power**, but not the **desire**, to do anything of Himself.
2. Subjection does not necessarily mean subordination.

II. ITS POSITIVE ASPECT .. .. .. ,, 19
1. **Not Imitation** of the Father.
2. "**What He seeth** (omniscience) the Father doing " (R.V.).

III. ITS BASIS .. .. ,, 20
1. **Perfect Love** flowing ever from One to the Other.
2. He was the **Unique Object** of the Father's Love.

IV. ITS MANIFESTATION .. .. .. ,, 20
Between the Father and the Son there are—
1. **No Secrets.**
2. **Perfect Understanding.**
3. **Perfect Communication.**

V. ITS DEMONSTRATION

1. **Quickening,**	..	..	..	..	..	verse 21
2. **Judging,**	..	..	..	..	..	vv. 22, 27
3. **Worship,**	..	..	..	..	..	verse 23
4. **Life-giving,**	..	..	..	..	..	vv. 25, 26

The Question. The question between our Lord and the Jews turned on His right to perform works on the day Divinely appointed for cessation from labour.

The Reply. Our Lord met their objections by—

(a) Claiming the right to do as His Father.

(b) God, when He ceased creating did not cease work. See R.V. of verse 17 : " My Father worketh *even until now.*"

(c) He carries on His works of Providence and Redemption without any Sabbath rest.

(d) God does not on the Sabbath day cease to communicate life to all things.

Our Lord's Work. Our Lord claimed that His unceasing work is as necessary to the world as the Father's work, or, rather, that He and the Father are together carrying out one work.

The Sacredness of Toil. When the Lord taught the love of God it startled mankind. But it was hardly less revolutionary when He taught that God works as well as God loves. A toiling God was repugnant to pagan people.

THE ADVOCATE AND JUDGE

Christ as Judge is a less familiar thought to many, than those aspects of Him as Sufferer, Saviour, Sympathiser, Shepherd, etc.

I. THE FATHER'S COMMITTAL .. .. verse 22

 1. For " committed " W. gives " entrusted."

 2. Distinction is between possessing and exercising the right.

II. THE MEANING OF THAT COMMITTAL

 1. More than the Judgment of the Last Day.

 2. Expression used in O.T. for " to rule."

 3. The whole work of the Divine government of the world.

III. THE OBJECT OF THAT COMMITTAL .. ,, 23

God will not receive adoration from one who refuses to honour the Lord Jesus.

IV. THE SUBJECTS OF JUDGMENT

 1. **Negatively.** Not those who have believed, .. ,, 24

 2. **Positively.** Those who have done evil, .. vv. 28, 29

V. A CHOICE 1 John 2. 1, or John 5. 22, 29.

Christ is Advocate now, or He will be Judge hereafter. These two are such absolutely different offices that it may surprise us to find one Person spoken of as performing the work of both. He cannot be *both at once*, but He can be one at one time and the other at another.

Advocate. We are in desperate need of Him, as we have broken the holy law of God. If the Lord Jesus is to be our Advocate, we must plead guilty. If we do not make Him our Advocate, He will become our Judge.

Those who Hear (verse 25). The spiritually dead now, and by and by the physically dead.

The Father's Committal (verse 22), means that the whole work of ordering, governing, and deciding the affairs of the world, the whole administration of the Divine government of the world, is put into the hands of Jesus Christ.

A WONDERFUL JOURNEY

The Passing from Death to Life through Christ the Life-giver

I. A STRANGE JOURNEY .. .. ..   verse 24
   1. **Unfamiliar.** The other journey from Life to
   Death is all too familiar to us by daily
   funeral processions. But not so the
   journey from Death to Life.

   2. **Present.** This journey takes place here and
   now.

II. A SWIFT JOURNEY .. ..   ,, 24
   "Is passed," not "is passing." "Only a step to
   Jesus."

III. A SIGNIFICANT JOURNEY
   This statement is significant in that it points
   out the difference between saved and unsaved.
   Which is nothing less than the difference between
   life and death.

IV. CONDITIONS NECESSARY
   1. **HEARING.** More than listening with the
      ears. It means hearing with the heart.
   2. **Believing** on God.

V. A SATISFYING JOURNEY .. .. ..   " Hath."
   The priceless possession of Eternal Life.

VI. PROOF OF THE JOURNEY .. ..   1 John 3. 14
   For a proof that we have undertaken the
   journey, see 1 John 3. 14.

Twofold Death. The death referred to here is of a twofold character :
(a) *Legal.* Sentence had been passed upon us, but not execution. The
sentence is now on account of faith reversed. (b) *Spiritual.* A spiritual
death. We ARE already dead, spiritually. Not a single spark of spiritual
life remains in us by nature.

WITNESSES TO CHRIST

Our Lord brings forth a fourfold witness to His claims to Deity

I. JOHN THE BAPTIST .. .. vv. 33-35

1. **Commendation.** The Lord describes him as a " burning and a shining light," or " Lamp " (R.V.).

2. **Significance.** " Burning," not smouldering.
   - (a) Activity.
   - (b) Reality.
   - (c) Thoroughness.

3. **Usefulness** of Light.
   - (a) *Pierces* the diseased eye and is painful. Such is the effect of truth upon diseased souls.
   - (b) *Illumines.* Guiding, Cheering, Comforting.
   - (c) *Saves,* by pointing out the way to safety.

4. **Price.** Such a life is costly. There must be a burning before shining. In giving light, the lamp itself is consumed.

5. **Enabling.**

6. **Reminding.**

II. HIS WORKS .. .. verse 36

III. HIS FATHER .. .. vv. 37, 38

IV. THE SCRIPTURES .. .. verse 39

Our Lord's Claims were indeed extraordinary. Now He turns to testimonies to the rightness of those claims.

His Own Witness. Care must be taken as to our interpretation of verse 31. To say, on the authority of these words, that our Lord's testimony about Himself was false, would be folly and blasphemy. He declared in chapter 8. 14 that His witness was true. He meant that they would say His witness was not true. This is exactly what they did subsequently say (see chap. 8. 13).

Man's Witness. Verse 34 means : " I do not depend solely on man's testimony."

Purpose. " These things I say," not merely to prove My Deity, but " that ye might be saved " for your own sake.

Chrysostom remarks : " He called John a torch, or lamp ; signifying that he had not light of himself, but by the grace of the Spirit."

SEARCH THE SCRIPTURES

Our Lord's own Testimony concerning the Holy Scriptures
of Truth

I. THE DUTY OF SEARCHING
The Passage taken as **Imperative**
1. Because of its Author.
2. Because of its Millions of Readers.
3. Because of your Own Soul.

II. THE NATURE OF SEARCHING
1. Search, not merely read.
2. As a lion or hound tracks by the scent.
3. Eager, diligent, painstaking, careful.

III. THE OBJECT IN SEARCHING
To find Him, the One True Object.

IV. THE PERIL IN SEARCHING
The Passage taken as **Indicative**.
1. **Ye Search.** They already were doing it.
2. **Ye Think.** They sought with a wrong object.
3. **They Missed Christ** in their search. We, too, may search the Bible, and yet miss Him of whom the Bible speaks.

Imperative or Indicative ? Translators and scholars inform us that this passage can be taken either imperatively or indicatively ; that either our Lord was urging them to search, or acknowledging that they already were doing it. Let us take both senses.

The Letter of the Scripture. The Jews honoured the letter of the Scripture, but neglected the spirit.

Why Search Elsewhere ?
" We search the world for truth ; we cull
The good, the pure, the beautiful,
From graven stone and written scroll,
From all old flower-fields of the soul :
And, weary seekers of the best,
We come back laden from our quest,
To find that all the sages said
Is in the Book our mothers read.—*Whittier.*

CHRIST AND UNBELIEF

Value of this Chapter. Viewed from a purely homiletic standpoint, and as this outline indicates, this chapter is valuable.

Searching Words. How searching are His words in verses 39 to 47. How pointed and pressing His words always are.

Want of Will. One reason why so many souls are lost (verse 40). Not merely because of men's sins, nor because of intellectual difficulties, but for *want of will*.

A Severe Indictment. "You do not really love God" (Weymouth, in verse 42).

A Prophecy. No less than 64 false Messiahs appeared to the Jews after Christ, and were more or less believed (verse 43). The readiness with which they believed these impostors was remarkable. But is it not so to-day ? There are many who prefer the extraordinary suppositions and imaginings of infidel scientists and philosophers, and the wild statements of Spiritists, to the plain, unadorned, sober statements of fact in the Bible.

A Cause. One principal cause of unbelief was that with all their apparent desire to hear and learn, they cared more in reality for pleasing man than God (verse 44).

Moses. The testimony of Moses is strikingly referred to in verses 45 and 46.

My Words. The Lord (in verse 47) deliberately assigns to His words authority equal to the Words of Jehovah recorded in the Old Testament. In the original 1578 edition of the Geneva Bible, the following are two of the verses printed on the first page :

> " Here is the spring where waters flow
>   To quench our heat of sin ;
> Here is the tree where truth doth grow,
>   To lead our lives therein.
> " Here is the Judge that stints the strife
>   When men's devices fail ;
> Here is the bread that feeds the life,
>   That death cannot assail."

FEEDING FIVE THOUSAND

The Miracle of the Five Barley Loaves and the Two Small
Fishes

I. THE GOSPEL

1. **Its Character.** Only barley bread, the food
of the poorest. Emblem of the plain,
wholesome character of the Gospel   ..   verse 9

2. **Its Sufficiency.** Sufficient for the needs of
all mankind. Philip thought of " a
little "—the Lord gave most abundantly   vv. 7, 12

3. **Its Addendum.**

(a) Comfort Considered. " There was much
grass "   ..   ..   verse 10
(b) Order Enforced. " Make them sit down "   ,,   10
(c) Grace Commended. " Jesus gave thanks "   ,,   11
(d) Thrift Encouraged. " Let nothing be lost "   ,,   12

II. HUMAN MINISTRY

1. **Needed by God.** The Disciples had the food
to distribute   ..   ..   ,,   11

2. **Inadequate without God.** The Disciples had
too little to distribute   ..   ..   ..   vv. 7, 9

3. **All-Sufficient with God.** The Disciples had
too much to distribute   ..   ..   ..   vv. 12, 13

After these Things (verse 1). This incident does not follow chrono-
logically upon the events narrated in the previous chapter. We must
insert between chapters 5 and 6, a journey from Jerusalem to Galilee, and
other events ; a period of nearly a year.

Five Thousand Men. Note it says 5000 men, probably women and
children being additional.

Sea of Tiberias (verse 1). John is the only Evangelist who calls the
Galilean Sea that he loved so much, by this stately term.

Philip belonged to the nearest town (John 1. 44), so the Lord appealed
to him (verse 5).

A Great Miracle. One of the Lord's most remarkable miracles. None
done so publicly. The only miracle related in the Gospels by all four
Evangelists.

Comfort Considered. Our Lord's thought for the bodily comfort of the
multitude is shown. The spot chosen was one where the soft and tender
grass of early spring abounded—ideal for sitting down.

Order Enforced. The distribution of abundant food to such a multitude by the disciples could only have been done by perfect order and
arrangement. What catering arrangements ever please us ?

Grace Commended. The giving of thanks before meat was publicly
commended by our Lord's example.

The Fragments (verse 12). R.V. has " broken pieces that remain over,"
i.e., not the scraps let drop by the multitude, but what was left unused.

Wrong Motives. Sheer curiosity drew the multitude, not a sense of
personal need (verse 2).

WALKING ON THE SEA

I. CHRIST'S CONTROL OVER NATURE

   1. **Walking on the Sea**   ..   .. verse 19
      Only God can tread upon the waves   Job 9. 8
   2. **Stilling the Tempest**   ..   .. verse 21
      Only God can control the winds   ..   Prov. 30. 4

II. CHRIST CARES FOR HIS DISCIPLES

   1. Disciples not exempt from toil   ..   Mark 6. 48
   2. Disciples not immune from trouble ..   .. verse 18
   3. Disciples not free from darkness   ..   ..   ,,   17
   4. Disciples not far from Christ ..   ..   ..   ,,   19

III. CHRIST'S COMING FOR HIS CHURCH

   1. **A Parable.** The Church now a tossed ship on a stormy
     sea. The Master absent in person.
   2. **A Prophecy.** The Master is coming soon ! His coming
     will end our troubles.

IV. CHRIST'S COMMAND OVER THE SHIP

   1. Christ arrives on board   ..   ..   .. verse 21
   2. The Ship arrives in port   ..   ..   ..   ,,   21

Unreal Display. Verse 15 shows the undesired result. The people were more concerned about the yoke of the Romans than the yoke of their sins. They were willing to accept Him as their King. He willed that they must first accept Him as their Saviour.

Unwilling Disciples. Evidently the disciples were unwilling—the language implies this—and Christ had to exercise His authority (Matt. 14. 23).

Loitering Disciples. The sail to Capernaum was one of six hours, but here they were only in the middle of the lake after seven hours' rowing. They must have loitered on the voyage discussing the miracle of feeding the five thousand just past. How dangerous is delay.

Christ's Comradeship. Verse 21 is not merely a miraculous ending of a stormy voyage, but surely is the unstudied statement of love's consciousness of a voyage shortened by Christ's presence and comradeship. After Christ came on board, such a grand time of fellowship had they, that before they knew where they were they had reached the harbour. His presence is everything.

FAITH

Christ's Philosophy concerning Faith

I. ITS ORIGIN
Faith is the work of God   ..   ..   .. verse 29

II. ITS NATURE
Faith is an act, not a sentiment, ... ,,   29

III. ITS TEST
Belief in Jesus as the Divine One   ..   .. ,,   29

IV. ITS BASIS
The Word of God   ..   ..   .. Rom. 4. 18

V. ITS OBJECT
Jesus Christ, the sent One   ..   .. .. verse 29

VI. ITS REWARD
Counted unto us for righteousness ..   Rom. 4. 3

A False Motive. What was the motive of their search for Jesus ? (verse 24). Christ exposes their false motive (verse 26).

A Good Place. They found Him in a good place—in the Synagogue (verse 59).

A Double Paradox. Verse 27 gives us a double paradox :
1. They should not labour for the perishable food which can only be secured by working.
2. They should labour for the heavenly food which is not to be earned by working.

In effect, this was a reproof of the common belief of labouring only for the things of time.

The Inquiry. His reference to working suggested their inquiry (verse 28). The people probably meant by the phrase " works of God," godly works. Our Lord's reply hints at a deeper thought.

The Act of Faith. Faith is a work, an act, not a sentiment. Not something that comes to a man apart from himself, and outside of himself. Faith is the exercise of our most inmost nature—an effort of the will.

Works and Work. Christ, in reply to their query (verse 29), uses the singular number and the definite article. They thought of works—a great variety of deeds and observances. He gathers them all up into one— This is THE WORK.

Faith's Object. The first act of all true working is trust—not in Jesus, but in Jesus as Christ, as the Sent One, as the Divine Son of God.

BREAD FROM HEAVEN

The metaphor, used in relation to the Lord Jesus Christ, has many valuable things to suggest to us

I. THE CROSS OF CHRIST .. .. .. verse 33
1. The Seed must die—Christ must
   needs die .. .. John 11. 47-53 ; 12. 23-33
2. The Wheat is cut down—Christ was cut off   Isa. 53. 8
3. The Grain is bruised and ground—
   Christ was bruised and oppressed .. Isa. 53. 7, 10
4. The Flour is baked in the furnace—
   Christ endured the fierceness of God's
   wrath .. .. Mark 15. 34

II. THE INDISPENSABLENESS OF CHRIST   vv. 32, 33
   Bread is a necessity of life.

III. THE HOMELINESS OF CHRIST .. .. verse 38
1. The Manna fell with the dew ..   Exod. 16. 13-15
2. Christ was meek and lowly .. .. Matt. 11. 29

IV. THE ACCESSABILITY OF CHRIST .. .. verse 37
1. The Manna lay around the host   Exod. 16. 13-15
2. The work of Christ is available for all   1 Tim. 2. 5, 6

V. THE APPROPRIATION OF CHRIST .. .. verse 35
1. He that **believeth**—**Faith** is the means.
2. Shall never **hunger**—**Satisfaction** is the result.

VI. THE INCORPORATION OF CHRIST .. .. verse 40
1. Christ shall dwell within us   Eph. 3. 17 ; Rev. 3. 20
2. We shall receive His own life.

Bread from Home. A soldier was given up to die, and his old father hastened from a long distance to his bedside in the hospital   He lay semi-conscious, and nothing that father or attendants could say would rouse him, until the old man said, "Here's a loaf of your mother's bread which I have brought you from home." "Bread from home," said the dying man, "give me some," and from that hour he began to mend. Bread from Home—that is what dying sinners need. Oh, may we, through God's help, hear many say, "Give me some."

Disparaging Remarks. How disparagingly they refer to our Lord's miracle of the previous day (verse 31).

A Contrast. The Lord corrects them (verse 32). Moses *gave*—a thing of the past. My Father *giveth*—an act of the present.

Appropriation of Faith (verse 37). Faith honours God by its trust, and God honours faith with His blessings.

Christ's Great Revelation. 1. I am the Bread of Life (v. 35). 2. All shall come to Me (v. 37). 3. To do His will, not Mine (v. 38). This is the Father's will (v. 39, 40). Life through the Son (v. 40).

Gazes On. Weymouth gives "gazes on" for "seeth" in verse 40.

TAUGHT OF GOD

God's Method of Drawing Men to Himself is by TEACHING, a
Method which—

I. HARMONISES WITH NATURE
1. Elements **attract** one another.
2. God **attracts** man to Himself.

II. ENNOBLES THE CREATURE
God draws man by the revelation of His knowledge (v. 44).
Man is therefore a rational creature, having mental
powers to take in the teaching (v. 45).

III. HONOURS THE WORD
God draws man by the message of His Word.
It is the sound of that harp that brings the stones of this
spiritual building together.

IV. GLORIFIES THE FATHER
God draws man by the Gift of the Word.
The greatest gift ever given was God's well-beloved Son.

V. EXALTS THE SON
God draws man by the Sacrifice of His Son.
Redemption through the Blood of Christ is the great
attraction of the Word of God.

VI. IMPOSES A RESPONSIBILITY
God draws man by the Sovereignty of His Being.
That God draws man by teaching, imposes the serious
responsibility upon man to listen to that teaching.
To ignore same is to despise God's sovereignty and
to flout God's will.

God's Method. Verse 45 must be read with verse 44. What is the
explanation ? Just this : God draws men by teaching. That at once
simplifies matters. The teaching of His Son, of His Son's disciples, of the
Word.

Secret Work. " Draw "—a suggestive expression, denoting the secret
work of Divine love in the heart.

The Tides. God loves to draw in nature. The tides are caused by the
drawing power of the moon. Evaporation, and in consequence the fer-
tilising shower, is the result of the drawing power of the sun. All nature
proclaims that God loves to draw.

Mental Powers. If He draws by teaching, then it proves that man is not
a block of wood or stone, that he is a rational creature, that he has the
mental powers to take the teaching.

Man's Duty. Bishop Hooper wrote : " God draweth with His Word,
and the Holy Ghost, but man's duty is to hear and learn ; that is to say,
to receive the grace offered."

Listened. " Every one who has *listened* to the Father" (verse 4, 5, *margin*).

EATING AND DRINKING

Eating and Drinking used as a Figure of Life in Christ

I. BEGINS BY DRINKING   ..   ..   .. verse 54

> Our Lord is speaking metaphorically, and de-
> clared in figurative language the necessity
> of our believing and relying on the sufferings
> and death of Christ as a Divine Propitiation.

II. ACQUIRED THROUGH DEATH   ..   ..   ,, 55

> His flesh and blood could only be available by
> death, therefore this figure of speech is sug-
> gestive of a way into life through death and
> sacrifice.

III. RECEIVED BY FAITH   ..   ..   ,, 56

> An act of faith, as definite as the reception and
> partaking of food and drink is necessary.

IV. SUSTAINED BY INDWELLING   ..   ..   ,, 56

> This life can only be sustained by the mutual
> indwelling of the believer in Christ, and
> Christ in the believer.

A Much Perverted Passage. Few passages have been so painfully
wrested and perverted as this.

Not the Lord's Supper. This passage does not refer to the Lord's Supper.
If this is to be understood literally as the Sacrament, then all the Roman
and English Catholic laity are lost, for only the priests drink the wine.

A Continuous Feast.   We must drink in over and over again, the
meaning of the Blood-shedding.

Abiding in His Presence. A person who abides in the presence of the
Lord Jesus Christ, in some mysterious way appropriates, unconsciously
and unavoidably, the life and character of Jesus Christ, so that he is built
up like Him.

DISCIPLESHIP TESTED

A Sorrowful Conclusion to the Famous Discourse of this
Chapter

I. DISCIPLESHIP EFFECTED .. .. John 1. 37

II. DISCIPLESHIP TESTED

   1. **By Persecution.**

      Many cease to follow Christ when perse-
      cution arises.

   2. **By Intellectual Difficulties** .. .. .. verse 60

      " Hard to take in " (Moffatt).
      " Hard to accept, who can listen to such
      teaching ? " (Weymouth).

III. DISCIPLESHIP ABANDONED .. .. .. ,, 66

   It would be strange indeed if God required of us
      depraved beings such things as were agree-
      able to us.

IV. DISCIPLESHIP STRENGTHENED

   1. **The Lord's Question** .. .. ,, 67

   2. **Peter's Reply** .. .. verses 68, 69

      (a) A sense of the all-sufficiency of Christ .. verse 68
      (b) A sense of the folly and danger of seeking
         elsewhere, ... ,, 68
      (c) A clear sense of the Lord's Deity .. .. ,, 69

A Sorrowful conclusion. Verse 66 is a sorrowful conclusion to this
famous discourse. It supplies a melancholy proof of the hardness and
corruption of men's hearts.

Hearing in Vain. Even when the Son of God was preacher many seem
to have heard in vain. Don't be surprised if you sometimes have failures.

History of Discipleship. Perhaps we can best consider these verses as
forming a history of discipleship.

Hard Sayings. Our Lord does not seek to tone down things. " If My
saying concerning eating My flesh offends you, what will you say when
you see that very Flesh ascending up to Heaven ? " (verse 62).

FEAST OF TABERNACLES

Seven Great Principles Enunciated by our Lord

The Time. Six months elapsed between chapters 6 and 7. Verse 1, "My time is not yet come." Five months were yet to run before the "time" of which our Lord spake was fully come, the time of the Cross (verse 6).

Reason of their Hate. They would have tolerated His opinions and statements if only He had not attacked their sins (verse 7). Verse 17 lays stress on "willing."

A False Witness. "He that speaketh *from* himself" (R.V. of verse 18). Speaking *from* himself, he will speak *for* himself, and *of* himself.

Knowledge. One secret of getting the key of knowledge is to practice honestly what we know. Living up to our light is the way to gain more light.

Public Recognition. "Nobody who aims at *public recognition* ever keeps his actions secret" (verse 4, M.).

GOSPEL IN MINIATURE

I. APPEAL
"If any man"   ..   ..   verse 37
1. **Christ Stood.** Attitude of a servant.
2. **Christ Cried.** Intense earnestness of a herald. A public proclamation.

II. APPETITE
"Thirst"   ..   ..   ,, 37
1. **Of Mind.** For Knowledge.
2. **Of Heart.** For Love.
3. **Of Conscience.** For Peace.
4. **Of Spirit.** For Holiness.

III. APPROACH
"Let him come unto Me"   ..   ..   ,, 37

IV. APPROPRIATION
"And Drink"   ..   ..   ,, 37

V. AFFLUENCE
"Out of him shall flow"   ..   ..   ..   ,, 38
1. Abundant **Purity.**
2. Abundant **Satisfaction.**
3. Abundant **Usefulness.**
4. Abundant **Freshness.**

VI. APPLICATION
Water, a fitting Emblem of the Holy Spirit   ..   ..   vv. 38, 39
1. **Plenteous.**
2. **Cooling.**
3. **Cleansing.**
4. **Quenching.**
5. **Fertilizing.**
6. **Refreshing.**

Occasion. During the seven days of the Feast, at the hour of morning sacrifice, water from Siloam was carried in a golden vessel, and poured out in memory of the water miraculously supplied in connection with the Exodus, and also in fulfilment of Isaiah 12. 3. The ceremony had just been completed on the last day, when there was a stir in the crowd, and a Man who had been watching stepped forward and said : "If any man thirst," etc.

The Spirit in John.   1. Regenerating (chapter 3).
                       2. Indwelling (chapter 4).
                       3. Satisfying for service (chapter 7).

ORIGINALITY OF CHRIST

At least six Things here show how Unique was the Lord
Jesus Christ.

I. HIS CHARACTER

Never *man* spake like this Man   ..   ..   verse 46
View Him only as a Man and He is an enigma.

II. HIS MATTER

No second-hand truth did He retail.

III. HIS STYLE

1. Simple and pictorial.
2. Great thoughts clothed in simple words.

IV. HIS MANNER

Gracious, yet firm.

V. HIS POWER

Mighty.   Went direct to the conscience.

VI. HIS SPIRIT

The spirit of His teaching was that of sympathy, kind-
ness, earnestness, and yet of humility.

Divided Opinions.   The people were divided in opinion about the Lord
Jesus (verses 40 to 43).

The Officers.   The constables of verse 45 must be those of verse 32.
How long they had listened to the Lord we know not, probably a day or
two.   *They were overawed by the majesty and power of Christ's words.*
They dared not lay hands on Him.   And now they return and preach
Christ to their unbelieving masters, declaring openly the effect of His
words upon themselves.   They were immensely impressed by Christ's
originality.

Foolish Reasoning.   What folly to judge any movement by the wealth
or intellectual standing of its followers (verse 48).

Lord Chatham.   We are told that those who listened to Lord Chatham
always felt that there was something finer in the man than anything he
said.   Accounting for the enormous power a certain preacher wielded, in
spite of lack of eloquence, a member of his congregation said : " There are
twenty years of holy living behind every sermon."

IN THE MIDST

I. THE SINNER .. .. verse 3

The world put a sinner " in the midst " in
order to condemn her.

II. THE SAVIOUR .. .. .. John 19. 18

God put His Son " in the midst " for the purpose of saving sinners.

III. THE SATISFIER .. .. .. John 20. 19

Christ came and stood " in the midst " in order
to bless His own.

Mistaken Notion. This incident is left out of many ancient manu-
scripts out of a mistaken notion that people might think the Lord encouraged this sin.

The Homeless One. Connect 7. 53 with 8. 1. He had no home but God.
He found rest and refreshment in communion with His Father.

Prayer First. Before entering into the Temple, He spent time in prayer.
Communion with God is a fitting preparation for the worship meeting, and
also for service (verse 2).

Worldly Righteousness. All the godliness some people seem to possess
is to find out other people's sin.

Bringing Sinners. Let us bring sinners to the Lord Jesus, but in a
different spirit, and for a different purpose. They brought her as a trap
to catch Him.

His Dilemma. If He said, " Let the woman die in accordance with the
Law of Moses " (Lev. 20. 10 ; Deut. 22. 22), they would have had a fair
ground on which they could frame a dangerous accusation against Him,
and would inform Pilate that this new King was actually adjudging life
and death. If, on the other hand, He bid them let the woman go free,
then He could be branded before the people as traversing the Law of Moses.

CONSCIENCE

I. ITS POSSESSION   ..   ..   verse 9

God's Ambassador in man to watch and protect His interests.

II. ITS LIMITATION
1. Conscience alone not a sufficient guide.
2. Requires enlightenment before it is followed.

III. ITS DANGER
1. Of ignoring it.
2. Of worshipping it.

IV. ITS REQUIREMENTS
1. Awakening.
2. Purging   ..   ..   Heb. 9. 14
3. Exercising   ..   ..   Acts 24. 16

A Silent Answer. Our Lord's first answer is silence (verse 6).

Why He Wrote. They had omitted Numbers 5. 23.

What He Wrote. Some Greek copies here read : " He wrote on the ground the sins of every one of them." " But He does not write men's sins on sand, but with a pen of iron and the point of a diamond, never to be forgotten till they are forgiven."

One Our Judge. Christ was without sin, and might have cast the first stone (verse 7).

Their Conscience. How was it that their consciences did not convict them before they entered the presence of the Pure One ? Our first duty is to enlighten our conscience before we seek to follow it.

From the Eldest to the Youngest. " Beginning at the *eldest* " (verse 9). Probably the eldest went out first because, having lived longest, he had more sins to remember.

" Go and Sin no More." Note how respectfully she answers the Lord (verse 11). He called her act " sin." He implies that the legitimate result of forgiveness is renunciation of sin.

Tradition. Tradition states that her name was Susannah, that she became a missionary to heathen women, and died in Spain.

LIGHT OF THE WORLD

I. CHRIST'S TESTIMONY

1. Concerning Himself.

(a) Light of the World   ..   ..   ..   verse 12
(b) Not Alone in Judgment ..   ..   ..   ,,   16
(c) Not Alone in Witnessing..   ..   .. vv. 17, 18
(d) Always Pleasing the Father   ....   ..   verse 29

2. Concerning His Followers ..   ..   ..   ,,   12
(a) Negative.
(b) Positive.

3. Concerning His Enemies.

(a) Ignorance of Himself   ..   ..   ..   verse 14
(b) Ignorance of the Father ..   ..   ..   ,,   19
(c) Wrong Judgment   ..   ..   ..   ,,   15
(d) Seeking in Vain ..   ..   ,,   21
(e) Unbelief and Death   ..   ..   ..   ,,   24
(f) From Beneath   ..   ..   ,,   23

II. CHRIST'S CLAIM   ..   ..   ,,   12

Viewed from Three Standpoints.

1. Evidential Value.

True to-day, though uttered nearly 1900 years ago.

2. Doctrinal Value.

(a) Messiah ..   ..   ..   Isa. 42. 6 ; 49. 6
(b) Visible Vehicle of Divine Presence.
(c) Implies Fall of Man.
(d) Universality of the Light.

3. Experimental Value.

He is the Life as well as the Light   John 1. 4

Occasion.   On the first evening of the Feast, two huge golden lamps, which stood one on each side of the Altar of Burnt-offerings in the Temple Court, were lighted as the night began to fall, and poured out a brilliant flood over Temple and City, while far into midnight troops of rejoicing worshippers clustered about them with holy dance and song.   Our Lord used this custom as a text for this great utterance.

Evidential Value.   This saying uttered by a Carpenter nearly 1900 years ago, is still true.   "As a matter of fact, He is the moral and spiritual Illuminator at this present moment of all the progressive nations on earth, and all who are not walking in His light are fallen into a state of stagnation and decay."

CONTINUANCE

The Value and Blessedness of Continuance

I. DEGREES OF FAITH

1. **Accepting.** Believing Him   (R.V.) ..   verse 31
   A mere acceptance of His claims, elementary but real so far as it went.

2. **Leaning.** Believing *on* Him   (A.V.) ..   ,, 30
   A further step, a weak person leaning hard upon Divine Strength.

3. **Reposing.** Believing *in* or *unto* Him   .. John 3. 16
   The rest of faith, bringing salvation, joy, and peace.

II. CONTINUANCE

A Message to those who have already believed   ..   ..   verse 31

1. **What to Continue In—**

   (a) His Word ..   .. verse 31
   (b) The Faith ..   .. Acts 14. 22
   (c) His Goodness   ..   ..   Rom. 11. 22
   (d) Prayer   ..   .. Col. 4. 2
   (e) Charity and Holiness   ..   .. 1 Tim. 2. 15
   (f) His Love ..   .. John 15. 9
   (g) Foundation Truths   ..   .. 2 Tim. 3. 14
   (h) Brotherly Love ..   .. Heb. 13. 1

2. **Reasons for Continuing—**

   It is a condition of

   (a) Discipleship   ..   ..   ..   verse 31
   (b) Fruitfulness   ..   .. John 15. 5
   (c) Power in Prayer ..   .. John 15. 7
   (d) Perpetual Comfort   ..   ..   .. John 15. 9
   (e) Perpetual Harmony   ..   ..   .. Heb. 13. 1

Continue. For " continue," W. gives " hold fast to My teaching."
Abide. " Abide " and " continue " are renderings of same Greek word.

BONDAGE AND FREEDOM

I. BONDAGE

1. **The Fact** .. .. verse 32
   Inferred by the reference to freedom.

2. **The Ignorance** .. .. ,, 33
   Sin blinds the mind to the fact of bondage.

3. **The Explanation** .. .. ,, 34
   All guilty, therefore all in bondage,

4. **The Result** .. .. ,, 35
   Degredation and servitude.

II. FREEDOM

1. **Hope for those in Bondage** .. .. .. ,, 35
   There is deliverance.

2. **Emancipation from Bondage** .. .. ,, 36
   The Person.
   The Promise.

3. **Secret of Deliverance** .. .. .. vv. 31, 32
   Continuance in His Word gives knowledge of
   Truth. This knowledge leads to freedom.
   The truth about—
   - (a) Ourselves.
   - (b) The Lord Jesus.
   - (c) The Holy Spirit.
   - (d) God Himself.

Seeking and Finding. "After all, what is better than *seeking* after truth ?" remarks some one. We know—*finding it.*

Degrees in Degredation. What a vast difference there was between the *condition* of Israel in Egypt, Daniel the Premier of Babylon, and the little maid (2 Kings 5. 2). Yet in *position* they were one, for they were all slaves.

Israel's Bondage. Verse 33. They find it convenient to forget the 300 years of captivity in Egypt ; the repeated captivities in the Judges, culminating in the 70 years' captivity in Babylon ; and that almost within sight of them the standards of Rome were waving over the Royal Palace. But they were not the last people who said they were free when they were not.

The Truth. The 20 C. Test.: " Truth with a capital T, suggesting Truth to be a Person.'

SATAN

I. HIS EXISTENCE
Not an imaginary being .. .. .. verse 44

II. HIS PERSONALITY
" He," not " It " .. .. „ 44

III. HIS BEING
A created one. " Creature " .. .. Ezek. 28. 15

IV. HIS ORIGINAL POSITION
" The cherub " .. .. Ezek. 28. 14

V. HIS APOSTASY
From a previous blessed state.

VI. HIS CHARACTER
" Murderer " .. .. verse 44

VII. HIS PURPOSE
The Fall of Man .. .. 1 John 5. 19 ; Eph. 2. 1, 2

VIII. HIS WEAPON
" The Lie " .. .. verse 44

IX. HIS PRESENT ABODE
The World .. Luke 10. 18 ; Job 1. 6 ; 1 Pet. 5. 8, 9

X. HIS DESTINY
The Lake of Fire .. .. .. Rev. 20. 10

" **Seed** " and " **Children.**" Observe difference between Abraham's seed (37) and children (39). See also Isa. 14. 12, 20 ; Ezek. 28. 11-19.

His Word personified (37).

His Knowledge. The power of knowledge derived first hand (38).

Their Descent. Christ's gentle hint as to their Satanic descent (verses 38, 39, 41).

One Proof of God's children (verse 42).

Satan's Progeny. Bad men are Satan's progeny (verse 44). " *Now worketh in* " (Eph. 2. 1, 2). But " *God worketh* in " His own (Phil. 2. 13). Satan imparts his wisdom and strength to the sinner, as God does to His own people.

Lies are Satan's chief weapon. By lies he slew Adam and Eve. " Father of *it*," *i.e.*, a special lie. See Luke 4. 5 and 6 ; 2 Thess. 2. 11

CHRIST AND DEATH

Our Lord's Antipathy and Glorious Emancipation from Death
He delivers from—

I. ITS STING
By His Blood Shed   .. .. 1 Cor. 15. 56

II. ITS FEAR
By His Grace   .. .. .. Heb. 2. 14

III. ITS LONELINESS
By His Own Presence   .. .. .. Psa. 23. 4

IV. ITS HOPELESSNESS
By His Resurrection   .. .. Prov. 14. 32

V. ITS DREAD
By renaming it   .. .. .. John 11. 11

VI. ITS SIGHT
By a Sight of Himself   .. .. .. John 8. 51

Dislike of Truth. If we paraphrase verse 45, it would be : " The reason why you do not believe Me is your thorough dislike to the truth of God."

Unanswerable Challenge. Note His challenge in verse 46.

Personal Abuse. Silenced in argument, these wicked men resorted to personal abuse, the common sign of a defeated cause.

Luther and Calvin. " Luther calls me a devil ; I will honour and love him as a servant of God," said Calvin (verse 52).

Christ and Death. Any casual reader of the New Testament is impressed with this, that " death is the one natural fact, the one human experience, to which Christ showed antipathy." " He groaned in the spirit " (John 11. 33), literally, " He was *indignant* in spirit." " While weeping for the bereaved, His holy resentment kindled at the ravages of the Destroyer, and all the dreadful havoc of the tomb which was spread out before Him " (chap. 11. 33 and 35).

Frances Ridley Havergal. " Shall never *see* death " (verse 51). In Memorials of F. R. Havergal : " Another Sunday evening, not able to go to Church, she searched into the meaning of John 8. 51, and her conclusion was, ' so when we come to die, our eyes will so really see Jesus Himself, that we shall not see death.' "

THE PRE-EXISTING ONE

Notice a Budget of Lessons on our Lord's Pre-existing Life

I. THE GOD-HONOURED ONE .. .. verse 54
There was no self-exaltation in Christ.

II. THE ETERNAL ONE .. .. vv. 56, 58
There never was a time when the Son of God
was not.

III. THE PRE-EXISTING ONE .. .. .. verse 56
The Old Testament Saints saw Christ's Day.

IV. THE JOY-BRINGING ONE .. .. .. ,, 56
The sight of Christ brings joy.

V. THE SORROWFUL ONE .. .. .. ,, 57
The ageing effect of sorrow.

VI. THE DIVINE ONE .. .. vv. 58, 59
Christ's Divinity forms a solid foundation for
a sinner's hope.

The Jews' Opinion. "Now we know you are mad and crazy, for no one except a person under the influence of a demon would make an assertion so opposed to the almost unbroken experience of mankind," is the meaning of verses 52 and 53.

Seeing and Tasting. Notice, they altered the Lord's words. He said "see," they said "taste." We can taste without seeing (verses 51 and 52).

Humility of Christ. How careful the Lord was to disclaim all self-exaltation. What He uttered the Father gave Him to speak ; if He had the keys of death, the Father had given them to Him.

Distinct Claim to Deity. Abraham had been dead and buried 1850 years, and yet he is said to have seen our Lord's day and (lit.) "leaped for joy." Here is a distinct assertion of our Lord's eternity. "If the mere dawn kindled such joys, what of the noonday ! "

Seven "I ams" in John's Gospel :

1. Bread (chap. 6. 35).   4. Good Shepherd (chap. 11. 25).
2. Light (chap. 8. 12).   5. Resurrection and Life (chap. 11. 25)
3. Door (chap. 10. 7).   6. Way, Truth, and Life (chap. 14. 6).
7. True Vine (chap. 15. 1).

SPIRITUAL VISION

I. THE LOSS OF SIGHT .. .. .. vv. 1, 2
A grievous matter. We " pity the poor blind."

II. THE RECOVERY OF SIGHT .. .. verse 7
At Jericho it was instantaneous, here gradual.
At Jericho a touch of Christ's hand, here
obedience to His word.

III. THE EFFECT OF SIGHT .. .. .. vv. 8, 9
A change of appearance, that even his neigh-
bours were uncertain as to his identity.

IV. THE RESULT OF SIGHT .. .. .. verse 34
The beginning of his joy was the commence-
ment of his sorrow.

Wash to See. "He washed...and came seeing." How strange! Wash
to see? I thought I had only to wash for cleansing! True, like Naaman,
we have to wash to be clean; but vision comes with the purity.

Symbol of the Spiritual. This is a message to those in mental and
spiritual darkness. And we have every right to treat it as symbolical,
for the Lord Jesus uses it to speak of spiritual blindness.

The Blind and Pity. The loss of sight is grievous. We " pity the poor
blind." Yet some blind do not want our pity.

" As Jesus Passed by He Saw." The marvel is that He saw anything
else but His own peril. He ever had a heart at leisure from itself.

The Blind do not in Every Case Realise their Sad Plight. Mark Guy
Pearse tells of once staying at a little village on the Cornish coast, and the
good man of the house sat on the settle by the fire. " I was anxious to
make his acquaintance, and seeing he was blind, I said with as much
sympathy as I could, ' Yours is a great affliction, my friend!' To my
astonishment he got up, and turned upon me angrily, and denied it utterly.
' No, it is not, said he, ' not a bit.' His wife hurried in to apologise.
' He always gets so angry. He thinks eyes are such stupid things.'" Not
the only blind person who acts in that fashion. Many poor blind sinners
treat the Lord's message and messengers thus.

PERSONAL TESTIMONY

I. ITS VALUE AND POWER

II. SOME HOMELY LESSONS

The Man's Replies. By a study of the man's replies we see how willing he was at first to give details of his healing (verse 11), but how weary he got, and how unwilling he became to go into details (verse 15).

How ? How ? Observe the repetition of "How ?" They could not get over the truth and fact of his healing, but they fell out about the mode.

Criticism. At the beginning he had hazy views. We never know how hazy our views are until we are well shaken up. Yet the way to become clear is to have a good shaking. We learn to thank God for criticism.

One Thing. Four "One things" of Scripture—

1. "One thing thou lackest,"   ..   Mark 10. 21
2. "One thing I know,"   ..   ..   John 9. 25
3. "One thing is needful,"   ..   ..   Luke 10. 42
4. "One thing I do,"..   ..   ..   Phil. 3. 13

Clay. "The blind man was made of clay, so clay was a good thing to mend him with.

How ! No small part of the disputes amongst men has been concerning the *mode* of the Spirit's working, and not the fact. But let us ever remind ourselves that each Person of the Blessed Trinity is Sovereign in working as well as in character.

COMPENSATION
FOR THE PERSECUTED

The Lord's Compassion towards and Compensation for the
Persecuted

I. THE COMFORT OF HIS PRESENCE ..   verse 35
As soon as His people suffer for His sake He
visits them and speaks words of comfort.

II. FULLER REVELATIONS OF HIMSELF ..   ,, 37
Christ makes up for all losses by a clearer
knowledge of Himself.

III. FIRMER ESTABLISHMENT OF FAITH ..   ,, 38
Resulting in the man's worship.

Excommunication. The dread of excommunication (verse 34) with a
Jew was second only to the dread of death, for it meant a living death.

The First Confessor. This man was the first confessor.

The Comfort of His Presence. Note verse 35. Apart from anything
He said, His presence was a comfort. Burkitt did not say too much when
he observed, " O happy man ! Having lost the synagogue, he finds
Heaven."

Christ's Severe Denunciation. Verses 39 to 41.

Ignorance and Guilt. Verse 41 does not mean that ignorance makes a
man entirely free from guilt. Many a one will have to answer for what he
ought to have known.

Our Lord's Self-Revelation. The Lord compensated this sufferer by
revealing Himself with extraordinary fulness. In no case but this and to
the Samaritan woman do we find Him so unreservedly declaring His own
Divinity and Messiahship. Remarkable is His method of comforting.
He comforts in a way no one else does. He gave this man a friendship
outweighing in value what he had lost. The compensations in each
Christian's life forms a wonderful study. He is never long in debt to any
one. He makes up for far more than we ever lose for His dear sake.

CHRIST, THE DOOR

I. THE JEWISH FOLD .. .. vv. 1-5

  1. **The Sheepfold**—The Jewish Nation, ... verse 1

  2. **The Shepherd**—Christ, ... ,, 2

  3. **The Door**—Natural Birth.

  4. **The Porter**—John the Baptist, ... ,, 3

  5. **Recognition—Many recognised Him as the True Shepherd,** .. .. ,, 3

  6. **Guidance**—Leadeth them out, ..., 3
      (a) Of Bondage.
      (b) Of Judaism.

II. THE CHRISTIAN FOLD .. .. .. vv. 7-9

  1. **Safety.** Shall be saved, ... verse 9

  2. **Liberty.** Go in and out, ... ,, 9

  3. **Satisfaction.** Life more abundantly, .. ,, 10

  4. **Fellowship.**

III. THE TRUE MINISTRY .. .. .. ,, 10
  The Under-Shepherds.

Three Parables. At first sight there seems a confusion of metaphors in this discourse on the Good Shepherd. Yet there is order and method. There are really three parables : (1) Fold (verses 1-10) ; (2) Shepherd (verses 11-18) ; (3) Sheep (verses 26-30). There are thus three distinct pictures drawn, and though similar figures appear in each, the central Figure is the same.

Universal. The Christian Fold, the Church. " If any man "—declares He is able to deal with the needs of every individual in the world.

Extent of Life. For " more abundantly," R. gives " above measure."

The Sheepfold. A few years ago a traveller noticed at Hebron that the sheepfolds were mere C-shaped walls. Inquiring why there were no doors, the shepherd replied, " I am the door," meaning that at night he lay wrapped in his cloak in the open entrance.

John Bunyan wrote : " Christ is the door that opens into God's presence, and lets the soul into His bosom ; and faith in Him is the key that unlocks the door."

THE GOOD SHEPHERD

The Most Popular and Comforting Metaphor or title of our Lord

I. HIS CHARACTER..   ..   ..   ..   Verse 11.

   1. **The Good Shepherd**, Dying, ...   John 10. 11

   2. **The Great Shepherd,** Caring, ...   Heb. 13. 20

   3. **The Chief Shepherd**, Coming, ...   1 Peter 5. 4

II. HIS KNOWLEDGE   ..   ..   ..   Verses 14, 15

   His knowledge of the sheep and their knowledge of Him is as deep, intimate, and effectual as the knowledge of the Father and the Son. This is a knowledge through—

   1. **Possession.** Ownership of us.

   2. **Affection.** Love for us.

   3. **Observation.** Looking at us.

   4. **Reflection.** Thinking of us.

III. HIS WORK

   1. **Gave His Life for the Sheep**—Sacrifice,   ..   verse 11

   2. **Giveth His Life for the Sheep**—Intercession,   ,,   15

   3. **Giveth His Life to the Sheep**—Indwelling,   ..   ,,   10

   4. **Calleth His Sheep by Name**—Interest in,   ..   ,,   3

   5. **Leadeth His Sheep**—Guidance, ...   ,,   4

   6. **Separates His Sheep**—Separation, ...   ,,   3

   7. **Unites His Sheep**—Care for, ...,   16

The Title. Perhaps our adorable Lord never gave utterance to a more fruitful word than this. Of all the metaphors and titles of our Lord none have become so popular, and none have conveyed so much truth and comfort to millions than this of the Shepherd.

Origin. Who first conceived of God as Shepherd ? Poor, wayward Jacob (Gen. 49. 24). Who first conceived of a king as a shepherd of his people ? (2 Sam. 5. 2).

Meaning. " *Good* Shepherd " means more than being kind-hearted ; it also means, " in every way efficient—in strength, skill, and tenderness."

The Hireling. What makes the difference between the Good Shepherd and the Hireling ? Just one fact—ownership.

How to Know Him. How to hear and know the voice of the Good Shepherd. In John Woolman's Journal we read : " I went to meeting in an awful frame of mind, and endeavoured to be inwardly acquainted with the language of the True Shepherd." " There was a care on my mind so to pass my time that nothing would hinder me from the most steady attention to the voice of the Shepherd."

OUR LORD'S COMING

John lays emphasis rather on our Lord's Words than His Works

I. ITS UNIQUENESS   ..   ..   Verse 10

    " **I am Coming.**" We have all been sent with-
        out any choice as regards our advent into
        this world.

    His coming into the world was a voluntary,
        conscious, freedom of choice.

II. ITS PREROGATIVE   ..   ..   ..   ••   ,, 18

        This was exercised regarding—

  1. **His Coming,**   ..   ..   verse 10

  2. **His Death.**   Voluntary,   self-determined.
    " Giveth," ..   ..   ,, 11

    Not dragged from Him by cruel men or cruel
        means. " No man," " I lay it down,"   ,, 18

  3. **His Resurrection** was in His own power,   ,, 18

III. ITS PURPOSE   ..   ..   ..   ••   ••   ,, 10

  1. **Life.** " That they might have life."

  2. **Abundant.** " And have it to the full " (M.).
    See also Luke 5. 32 ; Matt. 5. 17 ; Luke 19. 10.

IV. ITS REWARD   ..   ..   ..   ••   ••   verse 17

    How God values self-sacrifice.

The Father's Love. Verse 17 is a deep, deep word indeed. Here the reason of the Father's love is based upon the self-devotion of the Son. It is as if the salvation of mankind had called forth a new relation of love between the Father and the Son. At anyrate, that ineffable love was magnified and enriched. The fact of the Father's love remained with the Lord, supporting Him in His sorrow. Observe how God values self-sacrifice.

The Lord Came, not to be a mere teacher, not merely to introduce a new morality or a new ceremony, not only to be an example of holiness and self-denial; He came to bring life. He has life in Himself, being its foundation and mighty reservoir.

PLAINNESS OF SPEECH

The Jews asked for plainness of speech. The Lord replied so as to impress upon them their Ignorance as to their Poverty

I. POVERTY OF THEIR LANGUAGE   ..   ..   verse 25

Spiritual matter cannot be fully expressed in human language.

II. POVERTY OF THEIR OBSERVATION   ..   .,   25

There were evidences enough, but they were so wrapped up in their unbelief and pride that they were blind to them.

III. POVERTY OF THEIR DESIRE   ..   ..   „   26

They could not see, because they had no real desire to see.

The Time. " And it was at Jerusalem " (verse 22), suggests that an interval took place between verses 21 and 22, when the Lord was absent from Jerusalem.

An Impossibility. "Winter.' Dec. 18th. In his " Pilgrim Church," Ainsworth has a most original chapter on verse 24. " The underlying assumption of that plea was that the person and place of Jesus Christ could be summed up in a sentence, made plain in a few words, concluded in a brief, positive statement." But they were mistaken. " This plea betrayed ignorance of the true nature of spiritual knowledge, the most dreadful ignorance of life." You cannot compress fully spiritual things into human speech. Not one half has been told, because not only half can be told. " It is our duty to put a thing into a nutshell—if it is no bigger than a nut.'

Suspense. " How long dost thou kill us with suspense " (A. Clark) ; " hold us in suspense " (R.V., *margin* of verse 24).

Feast of Dedication. This was instituted by Judas Maccabaeus to commemorate the purification of the Temple from the three years' profanation to which it had been subjected by Antiochus Epiphanes, B.C. 165. It was held rather more than two months after the Feast of Tabernacles

CHRIST'S SHEEP

I. THEIR CHARACTER "Sheep"   ..   ..   verse 27
Weak, foolish, wayward, helpless, dependent.

II. THEIR MARKS   ..   ..   ,,   27
    1. **Ear-mark.** "Hear."
    2. **Foot-mark.** "Follow."

III. THEIR GREAT POSSESSION   ..   ..   ,,   28
    The Lord uses a figurative expression, "sheep,"
    which, like all His language, is full of
    meaning, indicating that as sheep are the
    weakest, most foolish, wayward, helpless,
    and most dependent of creatures, so is
    mankind.

IV. THEIR ABSOLUTE SAFETY   ..   ..   vv. 28, 29
    1. **Eternal** Life, which cannot end.
    2. **Divine** Promise. "They shall never perish."
    3. **In the Saviour's Hand**, from which none can pluck.
    4. **In the Father's Hand**, who is greater than all.

Comfort. These words have been an untold comfort to the saints. Persecuted, tossed about, yet immortal.

Melanchthon and Mycomurs. Melanchthon frequently quoted verse 28 in his letters, and in later years became his favourite Scripture. On the 4th March, 1546, soon after Luther's death, he wrote to Frederick Mycomurs Pastor of the Church at Gotha, who was very ill and near the end : " Dearest Frederick, those sweet words of the Son of God have often comforted me in great sorrows."

Eternal Perseverance. Surely we have the eternal security of the child of God here ! A learned Christian professor has stated : " I believe in perseverance, because I believe in the Scriptures and in the Sovereignty of God, and I believe in the Sovereignty of God because I see it in history and experience."

Luther has written a suggestive sentence : " The sheep, though the most simple of creatures, is superior to all animals in this, that he soon hears his shepherd's voice, and will follow no other. Also he is clever enough to hang entirely on his shepherd, and to seek help from him alone. He cannot help himself, nor find pasture for himself, nor heal himself, nor guard himself, but depends wholly and solely on the help of another."

THREEFOLD
SANCTIFICATION

I. CLEANSING OF BODY AND GARMENTS
See Exodus 19. 10, 14, 15.

II. PURIFICATION OF HEART AND MIND
From all moral defilement and filthiness of the flesh and spirit (2 Cor. 7. 1).

III. SETTING APART OF THE ALREADY CLEAN
For a definite and specific purpose (John 10. 36, with Eph. 5. 26, R.V.).

The Son's Oneness with God. What an amazing statement we have in verse 30. It means oneness, identity in will and character, not identity in person. The Father and Son are one in equality, nature, dignity, power, will, and operation.

The Father's Interest. Why has our Lord introduced this statement (verse 30) here ? In order to explain how it is that the Father should take as much interest in the sheep as the Son.

Our Lord's Defence. If princes and judges, who are merely men, are called gods (Psa. 82), He who is the Eternal Son of the Father could surely not be justly chargeable with blasphemy for calling Himself the Son of God ! Thus our Lord's defence of His own language against the charge of blasphemy is very remarkable.

Our Lord and Sanctification. Our Lord speaks of Himself as sanctified by the Father. This raises the question of sanctification. Note the Biblical threefold view.

Augustine, commenting on verse 30 and context, points out that this statement of our Lord overthrows Sabellianism, which says there is only one Person in the Godhead ; and Arianism, which says that the Son is inferior to the Father. Jesus declares He is ONE with the Father.

" Shewed " (verse 32). Do you detect the sarcasm in this verse ? " I have *shewed*" is an unusual phrase, meaning he had publicly exhibited before their eyes, and not performed them in a corner.

" The Scripture cannot be broken " (verse 35). Here is our Lord's view of the sacred Scriptures. Language could not be clearer or more emphatic on the pre-eminent authority of the Holy Book.

THE LOVE OF CHRIST

I. THE FACT OF HIS LOVE .. .. .. verse 3
This should be the first and uppermost thought
in our minds.

II. THE EXTENT OF HIS LOVE .. .. ,, 5
He loves **all**, in spite of diversity of character.

III. THE PERMITS OF HIS LOVE .. .. ,, 15
He loves, though He permits sickness and
suffering in our lives. And sickness is no
sign that God is displeased with us.

IV. THE DELAYS OF HIS LOVE .. .. 6 with 36
He loves, though He may delay in answering
our petitions.

V. THE ENIGMA OF HIS LOVE
He loves, though sometimes He seems to take
the best and leave the worst, *e.g.*, useless
lives prolonged and useful lives cut short.
Our duty is to trust, and at the last all will
be seen to have been not only *for* the best,
but really **the best.**

Bishop Ryle writes : " This chapter...is one of the most remarkable in
the New Testament. For grandeur and simplicity, for pathos and solemnity, nothing was ever written like it."

Three Lessons. Nowhere else shall we find such (1) striking illustrations
of our Lord's ability to sympathise with His people ; (2) such convincing
proof of His Divine power ; (3) and, at the same time, of His humanity
and divinity.

The Only Record. This miracle is recorded nowhere else.

Effect on the Rulers. The death of the Lord Jesus was finally deter-
mined upon as the occasion of His raising Lazarus (verses 46 to 53).

" **Bethany, the town of,**" etc. (verse 1). One of Robert M'Cheyne's
sayings is still remembered in Collace : " Bethany was known in Scripture
not so much as Bethany, but as the town of Mary and her sister Martha !
I wonder who in this place gives the name by which it is known in Heaven ?
It will not be known as Collace, but as the town of ——, perhaps some bed-
ridden believer."

" **Therefore** " (verse 6). Dr. Horton says : " There is no more amazing
conjunction in literature." There is a tarrying love as well as a succouring
love.

THOMAS

Three times only does Thomas speak in the Gospels, and each time it is with a sigh and a doubt

I. THE PESSIMIST   ..   ..   verse 16
From the records we judge him to have been a constitutional pessimist. Surely his faith at times died. Such deserve our pity.

II. THE FEARLESS   ..   ..   ,, 16
Though his tone is full of dolefulness, there is fearlessness regarding the results of following the Lord. It was he of all men who sought to revive the courage of the others.

III. THE LOYAL   ..   ..   ,, 16
What a complex character was his! With his pessimism and fearlessness there is a decided loyalty to his Master.

IV. THE CONTRADICTOR   .. John 14. 5
1. Pained Love, facing the black prospect of eternal separation. "We know not whither Thou goest."
2. Impatient Despair. "How can we know the way?"

V. THE BROODER   ..   ..   ,, 20. 24
Why was Thomas not with the company? He had slipped away full of sorrow and grief. He did the very worst thing a melancholy man can do—went away to brood in a corner by himself.

VI. THE WORSHIPPER   ..   ..   ,, 20. 28

The Proverb. It is difficult to say exactly what our Lord meant by the use of the proverb in verses 9 and 10
1. They had a working day of twelve hours.
2. "My working day is not yet over—until then I am immortal."
3. "The day—my day of work—is fast declining; therefore I must be up and doing." As one has said : "The Child of Eternity heard, with quickened ear, the muffled summons of the fleeting hours."

Walking in the Light. Did not these words suggest to John the idea of walking in the light developed in his First Epistle?

Thomas and Matthew. As he is always mentioned in the sacred lists with Matthew, he is regarded as Matthew's brother (Matt. 10. 3). By birth he was a native of Galilee.

THE RESURRECTION

Our Lord and the Resurrection

I. THREEFOLD CHALLENGE .. .. .. vv. 25, 26

1. **His Supernatural Character.**
   This is definitely asserted by our Lord.

2. **He is the Life.**
   He claims to be the Reservoir of Life.

3. **He is the Resurrection.**
   He refers to two Resurrections.

II. THE RESURRECTION OF THE DEAD

1. **Unknown to the Heathen**, though they believe in a future existence (Acts 17. 18, 31, 32).

2. **Known and Believed by the Jews** (Job 19. 25-27 ; Daniel 12. 2 ; and John 11. 24).

III. THE RESURRECTION FROM THE DEAD

1. **Unknown to the Jews.**

2. **First Clear Statement** by Paul (1 Thess. 4. 16).

3. **Second Hint** by Paul (1 Cor. 15. 51).

4. **Paul's Ambition** (Phil. 3. 11, R.V.).

The Disciples, encouraged by Thomas, accompanied our Lord to Judaea (verse 16).

Lazarus. Of course (verse 17) He knew Lazarus was dead beforehand.

Martha and Mary (verse 20). Characteristic actions, both reflections of their different temperaments.

Martha's Greeting. " Lord, if Thou hadst been here," etc. (verse 21)· Strange mixture of faith and reproof.

The Lord's Antipathy to Death (11. 33). " He *groaned* " (chafed, M.), literally, " was indignant," while weeping for the bereaved, His holy resentment was kindled at the ravages of the destroyer—death. He was never resigned to the reign of death. It is our Father's good pleasure to end that estrangement by and by.

He Delivers from Death's : (*a*) *Sting,* by His blood (1 Cor. 15. 56). (*b*) *Fear,* by His grace (Heb. 2. 14). (*c*) *Dread,* by re-christening it " sleep " (John 11. 11). (*d*) *Hopelessness,* by His resurrection (Prov. 14. 32) (*e*) *Loneliness,* by His presence (Psa. 23. 4).

THE TEARS OF THE LORD

Three Incidents of our Lord's Weeping are given in the Gospels

I. TEARS OF SYMPATHY   ..   ..   ..   verse 35

    On the Way to the Grave of Lazarus, at the
         sight of human sorrow, or because of the
         awful result of sin.

II. TEARS OF SORROW   ..   .. Luke 19.41

    Over Jerusalem, because of human perversity
         and stubbornness. Strange to weep at the
         very hour of triumph, amidst the plaudits
         of the people. He " *wailed*," for the word
         does not imply mere tears alone, so much
         as cries. But He saw the coming rejection
         of Himself and its inevitable results.

III. TEARS OF SUFFERING   ..   ..   ..   Heb. 5. 7

    In Gethsemane, because of the world's sin and
         its coming culmination in His crucifixion.
         Opinions vary as to the exact reason.
         Did He pray to be delivered from pre-
         mature death on account of great physical
         prostration ? or because of the fear of
         death ? Or was it because He knew of
         the separation from His Beloved Father
         when He died on the Cross ?

Weeping not Unmanly. The Persian, Xerxes, shed tears as he watched his vast army march past him on the way to Greece ; the iron Napoleon once melted as he reviewed the vast army which followed him to the disastrous Russian Campaign ; that manly man, Paul, wept at times (Acts 20. 19) ; but the highest type of manhood is to be found in the Lord Jesus, and He wept.

Shortest Text. The shortest text in the Bible is verse 35. The longest text in the Bible is Esther 8. 9, which sealed the doom of Haman, enemy of God's people.

THE RESURRECTION OF LAZARUS

A Parable in Action of the Quickening of a Soul from Spiritual
Death.　Note the various steps—

I. HUMAN IMPOSSIBILITY must be recognised　　verse 39
　　1. **Condition of a Man by Nature.**　Like Lazarus,
　　　　dead.
　　2. **Not a Spark of Life.**
　　3. **Corrupt.**
　　4. **Bound.**
　　5. **Helpless.**

II. DIVINE HELP REQUIRED .. .. ..　,, 34
　　　　So take the soul to the Lord Jesus Christ—
　　1. In your Prayers.
　　2. In your Preaching.
　　3. In your Lives.
　　4. By Personal Effort.

III. REMOVE OBSTRUCTIONS .. .. .. vv. 39, 41
　　1. In your Personal Life.
　　2. In Erroneous Interpretation of the Word.

IV. PRAYER AND PRAISE .. .. .. vv. 41, 42
　　　　This should always accompany any effort in
　　　　the presence of dead souls.

V. RELY UPON THE WORD .. .. ..　verse 43
　　　　It is the Word of God that is life-giving,
　　　　powerful, and sharper than any two-
　　　　edged sword. Let it be the Word itself
　　　　that is to do the work.

Awe-Inspiring Change.　There is nothing more remarkable in the
narrative than the contrast between Jesus weeping and indignant when on
His way to the grave, and the Lord serene, calm, majestic, and authori-
tative as He stands fronting the cave—sepulchre.　The sudden transforma-
tion must have awed the gazers.　He approaches the sepulchre as a cham-
pion preparing for a contest.

Progressive Manifestations of Divine Power.
　　1. The First Raised, ... Jairus' Daughter—just dead.
　　2. The Second Raised, .. Widow's Son—dead a few hours.
　　3. The Third Raised, .. Lazarus—dead four days.

A Parable and a Prophecy.　This miracle is a parable and a prophecy.
A prophecy of our own bodily resurrection ; a parable of the quickening
of a soul from spiritual death.　Observe, man had a part to play in the
raising of Lazarus (He refused to dispense with the assistance of man) ;
so also man has a part to play in the raising of dead souls.

THE DEATH OF CHRIST

Two Views of the Death of Christ are here brought out

I. THE WORLDLING'S VIEW .. .. .. verse 50

   1. Caiaphas spoke wiser words than he realised.

   2. The Jews hold in high regard any utterance
      of the High Priest.

II. THE DIVINE COMMENT .. .. .. vv. 51, 52

    In giving his judgment, it is remarkable that
      the words of Caiaphas contain the central
      doctrine of Christianity.

The Resurrection of Lazarus had raised a wave of popular excitement.
Any stir amongst the people was dangerous, especially at Passover time,
which was nigh at hand, when Jerusalem would be filled with crowds
of men, ready to take fire from any spark that might fall amongst them.
A hasty meeting of the National Council was summoned. A remarkable
testimony was given to the success of Christ's work. But the very thing
they dreaded they, by their own decision to put the Lord's Christ to death,
helped to bring about!

Caiaphas. How uncouth and unmannerly he was ! " Ye know nothing
at all." It is a brusque and contemptuous speech.

" It is Expedient." This word will always be associated in our minds
with Caiaphas. This word has its lawful time and use (John 16. 7 ; 1 Cor.
6. 12 ; 10. 23). In regard to truth, justice, and righteousness, the word
" expedient " should never be used. That which is morally wrong can
never become politically right.

Man's Short-sighted Judgment (48). Remarkable testimony to the
success of Christ's work. But the very thing they dreaded, and tried to
avoid when they put Christ to death, was brought about by that very action·

LOVE'S PRODIGALITY

Love always expresses itself in giving, and its gifts to God are—

I. GRATEFUL GIFTS
The expression of the soul's gratitude for His benefits. A cold heart and a stingy hand will generally go together.

II. LOVE'S GIFTS
The outpouring of a heart filled with love to the Lord.

III. WORSHIP GIFTS .. ..   verse 3
Giving is part of the true soul of worship. And Mary, in each of three references to her, is found " at the feet of Jesus."
1. **As a Humble Learner,** ..   Luke 10. 39.
2. **As a Bereaved Mourner,**   John 11. 32
3. **As a Grateful Worshipper,**   John 12. 3

IV. COSTLY GIFTS .. ..   ,, 5
A basin of water and a towel would have sufficed for the washing of her Lord's feet, but not for the relieving of her full heart. Her's was the type of love which gives its best.

V. FRAGRANT GIFTS .. ..   ,, 3
Refreshing to the Recipient, but perfuming the giver also, and spreading its fragrance through the whole house.

VI. ACCEPTED GIFTS .. ..   vv. 7, 8
All gifts offered the Master will be accepted by Him, though He does not judge them by their earthly value, *e.g.,* the widow and her two mites.

The Father and the Son. Have you noticed the distinctive work of the Father ? Jesus Christ " came to seek and to save that which was lost ; " the Father seeketh amongst the saved worshippers (Luke 19. 10 ; John 4. 23).

Worship should come before service (Luke 4. 8).

Three Suppers are recorded at the close of our Lord's ministry. (1) Six days before Passover (John 12. 2), His feet were anointed ; Judas did the speaking ; it was held in the house of Lazarus. (2) Two days before the Passover (Mark 14. 1, 3) ; His head was anointed ; the disciples did the speaking (Matt. 26. 8) ; and it was held in the house of Simon the Leper (Matt. 26 ; Mark 14 ; Luke 22). (3) The Passover Supper (John 13, etc.).

Judas' Calculation. Judas sold his Lord for £3 10/. Judas himself said Mary's gift would have brought from £9 to £10 in the market.

CHRIST AND THE ASS

The taking of the Ass and the Triumphal Entry into Jerusalem by our Lord were both unusual and parabolic

I. AN UNUSUAL ACT .. .. vv. 12, 13

1. **Courting Public Notice** was an unusual thing for our Lord to do. Yet here He deliberately brought about His public entry, acting in a way quite unlike His whole previous course.

2. **The Time had Arrived** at length for Him to declare His Royal Office. It was fitting that He should assert that He was their King before the hosts of Israel.

II. A PARABOLIC ACT .. .. verse 14

Our Lord's use of the ass has arrested Preachers.

1. **Our State by Nature.**
   - (*a*) Unclean.
   - (*b*) Without (Mark 11. 4).
   - (*c*) Bound.
   - (*d*) Untamed.
   - (*e*) By Two Ways.

2. **Our State by Grace.**
   - (*a*) Needed by the Lord.
   - (*b*) Loosed through the Lord (Rev. 1. 6, R.V.).
   - (*c*) Used by the Lord.

The Owners of the animal were probably secret disciples, with whom our Lord had arranged to send for it, and had settled a sign and countersign by which they would know His messengers.

In Levitical Days. The ass was associated with man in redemption (Exod. 13. 13). By nature man is associated with the ass, an unclean animal ; by wondrous Grace man is associated with the Lamb, a clean and sacrificial animal.

Lord Had Need of Him. Remarkable blending of dignity and poverty. His words assert sovereign authority and absolute right

SEEING JESUS

I. ITS PRIVILEGE
What a glorious privilege is this ! And by faith this privilege is still ours !

II. ITS POSSIBILITY
What the Greeks wanted was a private interview, for they could see Him publicly any time. But there is no record of their request being granted ; but we may, if we " look unto Him."

III. ITS QUALIFICATION ..   ..   verse 24
There is a modern cry, " Back to Christ." He would point us back to the Cross.

IV. ITS PATH
1. **By a Vision of the Spirit** (1 Cor. 2. 10-14).
2. **Through the Eyes of the Mind** (Eph. 1. 18 ; cp. Eph. 4. 18).
3. **Through the Heart.**

V. ITS OBSTACLES
There are always obstacles, Zacchaeus was too small, Bartimaeus was blind, etc.

VI. ITS PROGRESSIVENESS
" **Looking,**" present tense, " unto Jesus " (Heb. 12. 2).

VII. ITS FRUIT
" They looked unto Him and were radiant " (Psalm 34. 5, Am. R.V.).

Came Up. (1) Worshipping is often uphill work. Many things conspire to hinder us from the quiet hour. (2) The worshipping spirit needs cultivating. (3) Waiting on God is a rare exercise of soul.

Philip. (1) Why they came to Philip in preference to the others we know not. (2) It has been conjectured that Philip, being an inhabitant of a town in North Galilee, near Tyre and Sidon, was more likely than the other disciples to be acquainted with Greeks.

CHRIST GLORIFIED

Oh! what shame there was in the Cross! But Heaven
viewed the Glory in the Shame

I. IN HIS SUFFERING

The suffering revealed the glory of His character, bringing
out more clearly—

1. **His Obedience** to the Will of God.
2. **His Love** for Sinful Man.
3. **His Utter Unselfishness.**
4. **His Faithfulness** to His Obligations.

Thus was the *Man* revealed, and a man's real glory is not
in what he *has* or *does*, but in what *he is*.

II. THROUGH HIS SUFFERINGS

The Cross of Christ not only revealed the beauty of His
character, but gave Him His supreme place.

" **Wherefore** God also hath highly exalted Him " (Phil.
2. 9). The glory of Saviourhood became His through
the Cross, and the glory of a great triumph will
become His by and by.

" **Saw His Glory.**" Is there not a mistake? Should it not be shame?
That is how we would view it. Certainly there *was* shame in the Cross·
But Heaven views things differently.

The Glory of the Cross. Without doubt when the Lord and Isaiah spake
of glory it was His dying of which they were thinking (see John 7. 39).

The Hour is Come. Surely His words imply that the hour had struck
when His real and essential glory was to flash out upon a startled and
astonished world. Up to this point His glory had been veiled, though
glimpses had been given. " We beheld His glory " (John 1. 14). " Manifested forth His glory " (John 2. 11)

" **Now is my soul troubled** " (verse 27). " Now is my soul full of trouble "
(W.). " Now I am troubled at heart " (20 C.).

" **What shall I say?** " Perplexity.

An Unglorified Christ (John 7. 39). The water of life would not flow
until the Rock was smitten. The fact of an unglorified Christ is proof of
the absence of the Holy Spirit.

THE SON OF MAN

A unique expression seldom found upon the lips of any but our Lord. No one ever called Him this whilst He was here in the flesh, and only thrice is it used of Him by others after His Resurrection (Acts 7. 56 ; Rev. 1. 13).

I. THE REALITY OF HIS INCARNATION

1. **Identifying** Himself with us.

2. **Declaring** reality of Incarnation.

3. **Emphasising** His Humanity.

II. THE SUPREMACY OF THE LORD

1. **Unique Relationship** to the world, distinguishing Himself from us.

2. "**The** Son of Man," gathering up in Himself all the qualities that constitute the perfect Ideal of Manhood.

The Head of the Son of Man is first mentioned in the New Testament in Luke 9. 58, and the last time in Rev. 14. 14　What a glorious contrast.

Sundry Lessons suggested by our Lord s use of this phrase, Son of Man.

1. By it our Lord distinguished Himself from us, plainly claiming a unique relationship. How absurd it would be for any of us to be repeatedly insisting on the fact that He was a man, for that is only too evident. Here is emphasised the reality of His manhood, and yet its uniqueness.

2. This title, when used by Christ, always has the definite article. I am A son of man ; He is THE Son of Man, the best Man that ever lived.

3. It is particularly a title connected with the earth. As Son of God He is "the Heir of all things" (Heb. 1. 2); as Son of Man He is Heir to the dominion in the earth, which was entrusted to and lost by the First Adam, but regained by Christ the Last Adam.

UNDEVELOPED LIVES

The Secret of Fruitfulness ; or, Crucifixion comes before Coronation

I. THE TRAGEDY

" The tragedy of early death is not its suffering, but the blighted promise. The little casket full of latent possibilities is shivered to atoms."

1. In the Vegetable World.
2. In the Physical World.
3. In the Spiritual World.

II. THE REASON

Our Study points to one reason why lives of gracious promise are blighted and undeveloped. In every corn of wheat that finds no congenial soil there are undeveloped possibilities of harvest, and in every Christian life that has not responded to the congenial soil it is hidden in (" hid with Christ in God ") there are undeveloped possibilities of harvest.

III. THE CORN OF WHEAT

1. **Symbol of our Lord.** The simple request of the Greeks was as a narrow window through which the Lord's yearning spirit saw a great expanse. Nothing less than the coming to Him of myriads of Gentiles, the " much fruit " of which He speaks. But before that could take place, death on the Cross must be His. And this is the great law in nature and in grace ; in plants and seeds, life comes by death.

2. **Symbol of His People.** For five centuries the Greeks had marched at the head of humanity. The whole world gathered round the torch of Greek genius. Yet they failed to regenerate society. Why ? " Their master-words were self-culture and self-enjoyment. But Christ calls upon us to substitute self-oblation for self-culture, self-sacrifice for self-gratification."

IV. THE SECRET OF USEFULNESS

1. **In Christ** as our Soil.
2. **Surrender** to our Environment.

THE VOICE FROM HEAVEN

I. THE LORD .. .. vv. 27, 28
1. **Trouble of Soul** often follows great exaltation of Spirit, but is not necessarily sinful. "Now is my soul troubled." These utterances tell of a struggle within, a sudden, strong, mental, and spiritual agony. It was a struggle arising from the natural feelings of One who was perfect Man, and as man could suffer all that man is capable of suffering.
2. **Perplexity of Mind.** "What shall I say ? "
3. **Recognition of Divine Plan.** "For this cause."
4. **Consuming Passion for God's Glory.** "Father, glorify Thy Name."

II. THE VOICE .. .. verse 28
1. **Thrice Heard.**
   (a) At His Baptism.
   (b) At His Transfiguration.
   (c) At this Time.
2. **Significance.**
   (a) Proof that the Father and Son are two distinct Persons in the Godhead.
   (b) Intimate relationship between Father and Son.
   (c) Unbroken communion between Father and Son, though the Son was here in the flesh.
   (d) The Approval of the Father in the Son.
     (1) On the 30 years' obscurity before His Baptism.
     (2) On His early ministry to His transfiguration.
     (3) On all His earthly ministry and on His coming Passion.

III. THE PEOPLE .. .. vv. 29, 30
1. **Attempt to Explain** away the supernatural ("Thunder").
2. **Fail to Recognise** the Voice of God ("Angel").

Ears to Hear. How differently to different persons the voice of God sounds : (1) According to the state of heart, and (2) according to the keenness of spiritual hearing.

THE GREAT MAGNET

I. THE MAGNET ITSELF   ..   ..   ..   verse 32

The Great Magnet is not the Cross, nor the Gospel Story, but the Lord Jesus Christ Himself through and in the Gospel Story.

II. THE MAGNETISM   ..   ..   „   33

The Christ who was lifted up on the Cross is the Christ who draws men.

1. **The Appeal of Suffering** always strangely moves us.

2. **The Appeal of Sympathy.** Suffering for the sake of others specially moves us. And this is even more so when the appeal of the vicarious suffering of the Saviour is made.

3. **The Appeal of Individual Testimony.** Nothing so overcomes a man's will and reason as the preaching of Jesus Christ and His Cross.

4. **The Appeal of Human History.** " No one ever moved multitudes like the men with the magnet of the uplifted Christ."

A Mistake. A famous preacher remarked : " There is no driving in anything which pertains to God ; it is Satan that drives ; God persuades, draws." But it is not exactly correct.

Driving and Drawing. God both drives as well as draws. His drivings invariably are mentioned in connection with Judgment (Gen. 3. 24 ; 4. 13, 14 ; John 2. 13-16), whilst his drawings are in connection with salvation (Gen. 49. 10 ; Song of Sol. 1. 4 ; John 6. 44 ; 12. 32).

Last Public Utterance. Verses 35 and 36 form the last words of our Lord's public ministry, for afterward He only addressed His own.

The Great Magnet. Oh, Christian workers, ever lift Christ up. Speak of His death, and not merely of His life. You demagnetise Christianity, as all history shows, if you strike out the death on the Cross for a world in sin. What is left is not a magnet, but a piece of scrap-iron.

What is the Gospel ? Look at 1 Corinthians 15. 1 to 3 : " Christ died for our sins...was buried, and that He rose again the third day."

WASHING THE DISCIPLES' FEET

The Lord had closed His ministry to the world, but before He could have deep, deep communion with His own, there must be cleansing. He is here revealed in a threefold office.

I. THE CLEANSER OF THE SOUL .. .. vv. 8-10
   1. Our Desperate Need. Uncleanness of—
      (a) Walk. " Feet."
      (b) Work. " Hands."
      (c) Thought. " Head."
   2. Necessity of Cleansing, or " no part " in Him,   verse 8
   3. The Type. The Laver.

II. THE PURIFIER OF THE LIFE .. .. verse 10
   1. Necessity. Because of daily defilement of the way.
   2. Cleansing. By " the water of the Word."

III. THE PATTERN FOR HIS OWN .. .. vv. 13-17
   Christ is revealed as the Model Servant, an example of—
      1. Humility.
      2. Self-Denial.
      3. Service.

IV. REFLECTIONS OR LESSONS
   1. Cleansing comes before communion.
   2. A knowledge of one's end, ... verse 1
   3. A departing to the Father—a charming expression, ... ,, 1
   4. Loving to the uttermost—" unto the end," .. ,, 1
   5. Satan busy at the feast, ... (R.V.) ,, 2
   6. Time the great interpreter, ... ,, 7
   7. What to call the Lord, ... ,, 13
   8. Another beatitude, ... ,, 17

Loving " to the uttermost." (R.V.) " Unto the end." Why, there is no end to love ! The R.V. expresses the depth and degree, rather than the limitations of Christ's love

The Cleansing of the Soul. That this ceremony was emblematical of a spiritual cleansing was not recognised at first, not even by Peter. But when Peter saw what our Lord meant he became most enthusiastic. Peter's urgent request was in reality his confession of utter uncleanness, as if he had said : " I have sinned in thought (head), work (hands), as well as in walk (feet)." That is true of all. Our heads have conceived many a sinful thought ; our hands are guilty of many offensive actions ; our feet have often wandered into sinful paths. Though the bathing of regeneration can never be repeated, yet we need a daily cleansing.

JUDAS

The Tragedy of a Lost Life

I. ASSETS

1. Tribe of Judah.
2. Called by the Lord.
3. Business Abilities.
4. In the Presence of the Lord Jesus.
5. Feet Washed by the Lord.
6. Partook of the Last Supper.

II. GROWTH OF SIN

1. Love of Money.
2. Stole (John 12. 6).
3. Listened to Satan (John 13. 2).
4. Hypocrisy. He was not suspected by the Eleven.
5. Possessed by Satan (verse 27).
6. Betrayal.
7. Remorse.
8. Suicide.

III. LORD'S APPEAL TO JUDAS

1. Warning Appeal against Mammon (Matt. 6. 19).
2. Warning that he was Discovered (verse 21).
3. Act to Show he was Still Loved (verses 26, 27).

IV. RESULT

" And it was night " (verse 30). True in both natural and spiritual sense.

Sad Sights. One can never gaze upon a wreck at the seaside without strange, sad reflections. It is a sadder sight to gaze at a ruined body and a wrecked soul, especially if that one, as in the case of Judas, has had unparalleled opportunities.

Growth of Sin. Note the awful growth of sin in Judas. He had a love of money and he gave way to it, appropriating money that did not belong to him. He then entertained the suggestions of Satan. Let us remember that no one suspected him, hence he was a successful hypocrite. Then he became possessed by Satan (verse 27), and soon betrayed his Master, ending in remorse and suicide.

THE LIVERY OF CHRIST

Our Lord's New Commandment on the eve of His Departure.

I. A NEW BOND .. .. vv. 33, 34
  1. **His Presence had held them together** up to now.
  2. **But He was about to leave them.** What then ?
  3. **He introduces a new bond,** the bond of love,
     which was now to unite them as one.

II. A NEW OBJECT .. .. verse 35
  The Jew was a partizan, loving only the Jew
  and hating the Gentile. Here was a new
  object, " all."

III. A NEW MOTIVE .. .. verse 34
  "I have loved." We love because He first
  loved us.

IV. A NEW STANDARD .. .. verse 34
  "As I have loved you." Loving one another
  was a command at least 1400 years old
  (Lev. 19. 18 ; Deut. 10. 19). But its new-
  ness lay in this new standard. His was a
  love that emptied itself, humbled itself,
  sacrificed itself, and had no thought of
  self.

V. A NEW LIVERY
  " As every lord giveth a certain livery to his
  servants, *love* is the livery of Christ "
  (Latimer).

VI. A NEW ENABLING .. .. John 17. 9
  The love we need is God Himself coming into
  the heart, taking possession of our whole
  soul, and filling it with His love, because
  He has filled it with Himself.

Illustration. One Saturday evening Samuel Rutherford's household
were gathered together for their devotions, when a knock was heard at
the outer door. A stranger sought admission. He was welcomed, and
took his place in the circle of those who were there answering the various
questions of the Catechism. It so chanced that the question, " How many
commandments are there ? " came to the newcomer, as the one to which
he was to make reply, and instantly he answered, " Eleven." Rutherford
sternly rebuked him. " A New Commandment I give unto you," etc.,
the stranger replied, who turned out to be Archbishop Usher, Primate of
Ireland.

AFTERWARDS

The occurrence of the words " hereafter " and " afterwards " is very impressive. Here are some of God's " afterwards."

THE AFTERWARDS—

I. OF RECONCILIATION		..	..	.. Gen. 32. 20
II. OF FOLLOWING	..	..	..	John 13. 36
III. OF SERVICE ..	..	..	..	.. Exod. 5. 1
IV. OF KNOWLEDGE	..	..	..	.. John 13. 7
V. OF SUFFERING	..		Heb. 12. 11 ; Gen. 15. 14	
VI. OF GUIDANCE	..	..	..	Psalm 73. 24

Peter's Characteristics are all in operation here :
1. Eagerness to be in the front.
2. Habit of blurting out his thoughts and feelings.
3. Passionate love for his Master.
4. Inability to understand Him.
5. Self-confidence.

To Follow Christ means to die daily, moment by moment, slaying self, suppressing self, abjuring self.

The Difference of our Lord's Word to His enemies (John 7. 34) and to His own (John 13. 36).

Before Peter could Die for his Lord, his Lord must die for Peter ; before Peter could die for his Lord, he must first die to himself ; and Peter must also die to the world. He felt he could have gone to the death, but he could not stand being laughed at. " He would have been ready to meet the executioner's sharp sword, but the servant girl's sharp tongue was more than he could stand."

Glory of Christianity is that it sets before us, instead of obedience to a precept, as other religions, the following of a Person (verse 36).

What he should have said. " Lord, *thy grace enabling me*, I will lay down my life for Thy sake." The world deems self-confidence a condition of success and power ; but the Lord and His Word clearly teach it to be the root of weakness, and the secret of abject failure.

A QUIET HEART

One secret of a Quiet Heart is given in this verse, and two thoughts are prominent, heart and faith

I. HEART

  1. **Oneness of Heart** (not " hearts "). What a glorious unity was theirs !

> (a) Loving the same Lord.
>
> (b) Enshrining the same Word.
>
> (c) Indwelt by the same Spirit.

One with one another because one with Him.

  2. **Restfulness of Heart.** " Not troubled."

  3. **Responsibility of Heart.** " Let not." " Keep thy heart with all diligence."

II. FAITH

> Faith is the secret of tranquillity.

  1. **Recognised.** " Ye believe in God." Christ recognised their faith.

  2. **Enlarged.** " Believe also in Me." Christ points to Himself as the Object of precisely the same trust as that which is given to God.

  3. **Fruitful.** The Bible perpetually associates rest of heart with strength of faith.

The Setting. " The twelve were sitting in the upper chamber, stupified with the dreary, half-understood prospect of Christ's departure. He, forgetting His own burden, turns to comfort and encourage them. These sweet and great words most singularly blend gentleness and dignity. ' Let not your heart be troubled.' Oh, the cadence of soothing tenderness ' Believe in Me.' What a tone of majesty ! '

Responsibility. It is clear from our Lord's words, "*Let not* your heart be troubled," that we are responsible for the condition of our hearts. The power to keep our hearts tranquil is at our hand. Here is the secret of tranquillity—faith in God and His Christ. Faith in God and faith in Christ are not two, but one. Faith in God which is not also faith in Christ is imperfect, and has no saving element in it.

HEAVEN, A HOME

" In My Father's House." Heaven is a homely place.

I. WITHOUT A SHADOW

1. Of Sin, ..	..	..	..	..	Rev. 21. 27
2. Of Sorrow,	..	..	..	..	Rev. 7. 17
3. Of Removal,	..	..	..	..	Heb. 13. 4
4. Of Need, ..	..	..	..	..	Rev. 7. 16, 17

II. OF HOLY LAUGHTER

It is called in New Guinea " the place of laughter," from their custom of sitting after supper, and laughing over the happenings of the day. It will be a place of many little children.

III. OF REST (Rev. 14. 13).

IV. OF LIGHT (Rev. 21. 22-25 ; 22. 5).

V. OF ADORING WORSHIP (Same word for Temple, John 2. 16).

VI. OF HAPPY SERVICE (Rev. 22. 3).

VII. OF BLESSED RELATIONSHIP " *Father's* House "

Pilgrim Marks. Lord Rothschild is perhaps one of the richest men in the world. Those who have visited his home say it is lovely. But in the midst of splendour and perfection there is an unfinished cornice. He is an orthodox Jew, and every Jew's house, according to tradition, has some piece unfinished, to bear testimony that the occupier is but a pilgrim here. The unfinished cornice says : " This is not my home ; I am travelling to Eternity ! " Are there any pilgrim marks in your home, and life, and conduct ?

A Home of Rest. A little girl was stricken with fever, and for many days and nights the mother watched by the child's crib. At last the doctor said the child was dying. The mother took the little one in her arms, and began to tell her about the City she was so soon to see, of the golden streets and gates of pearl. But the child cried : " I'm too tired, mother, and I don't care to see all those things." Then the mother told of the beautiful music, and how the angels sing, but the child said, " Oh, mother, I'm too tired to hear all that beautiful music." The poor disappointed mother gathered the little one closer to her, and the child exclaimed, " That is what I want. Do you think Christ will take me in His arms, and let me rest ? " " Yes, my child," sobbed the mother, " He shall gather the lambs with His arm, and carry them in His bosom."

REVELATION OF THE FATHER

I. HUNGER FOR THE FATHER   ..   ..   verse 8

This outburst of Philip, by which he interrupted the calm flow of our Lord's discourse, was not the product of mere frivolity or curiosity, but a revelation of real heart-hunger. The longing was not merely to know God, but God as Father. We begin our spiritual childhood by a knowledge of the Son, and one mark of spiritual maturity is a knowledge of the Father.

II. RECOGNITION OF THE FATHER   ..   ,,   9

" Hast thou not *recognised* (20 C.) Me ? " It is possible to be much in a person's company and yet not know them. " So long time." Philip was one of the earliest disciples. " So long . . ." There is weariness, keen regret, pathetic longing, in that expression.

III. REVELATION OF THE FATHER

A Son can reveal his Father—

1. **By his Image.** Being like him in face and body.
2. **By his Disposition.** Like him in likes and dislikes.
3. **By his Words.**
4. **By his Actions.**

Our Lord revealed the Father in the last three particulars. But in Christ we have more than a symbol, He was the " express image " (Heb. 1).

IV. HONOURING THE FATHER

If one would honour the Father, he must fulfil certain conditions.

1. **Come to the Son** (verse 6).
2. **Love the Lord Jesus Christ** (verse 23).
3. **Separation** from sin and the world (2 Cor. 6. 17, 18).

It is one thing to be the father *of* a child, and another to be a father *to* a child. God is the Father of all who believe on the Lord Jesus, but all the fatherliness of His heart can only be revealed to the separated one.

THE HOLY SPIRIT

The Father's Second Greatest Gift

I. HIS PERSON

1. **A Person,** not a mere influence (John 16. 13, 14).
2. **Proceedeth from the Father** (John 15. 26).
3. **Given in Response to Saviour's Intercession** (verse 16).
4. **Hating Unreality** (verse 17).

II. HIS WORK

1. **In the World** (John 16. 8 to 11).
   - (*a*) Reproving.
   - (*b*) Convicting.
   - (*c*) Convincing.

2. **In the Church.**
   - (*a*) Strengthening (verse 16).
   - (*b*) Illuminating.
   - (*c*) Revealing (verse 26).
     - He loves the Truth.
     - He reveals the Truth.
     - He applies the Truth.
   - (*d*) Teaching (verse 26).

The Doctrine. " Sometimes friends ask me to recommend them a book upon the Holy Spirit. My reply is, ' Read John's Gospel, chapters 14 to 16 ; for there you have weighty statements concerning the Holy Ghost from the lips of the Master Himself ' " (Dr. Campbell Morgan).

Order of Experience. (1) "Believe " (verse 12), then (2) Love (verse 15).

Asking and Commanding. There is a connection between verses 13 and 15. The Lord does as the sinner asks ; the servant does as the Lord commands.

Cause and Effect. " If ye love Me *ye will* keep My commandments " (verse 15, R.V.).

Paradoxes in verse 19 : Absent, yet present ; unseen, yet visible ; dying, yet ever living.

Two Advocates. Christ *for* me at the Father's right hand (1 John 2. 1) ; the Holy Spirit *in* me for the Father.

NOT AS THE WORLD GIVETH

The Giving of Christ is Contrasted with that of the World

I. THE WORLD GIVES

1. **False Peace,** by closing the eyes to sin.
2. **Outward Peace,** which changes with circumstances.
3. **According to Deserts.**
4. **Niggardly.**
5. **Grudgingly.**
6. **With Ulterior Motives.**
7. **Soon its Last Gift.**

II. CHRIST GIVES

1. **Real Peace by the Blood,** by opening the eyes to sin and revealing Himself as Saviour from it.
2. **Inward Peace,** through His indwelling Presence.
3. **According to Grace.**
4. **Abundantly.**
5. **Gladly and Willingly.**
6. **For the Recipients' Sake Only.**
7. **Continuously.**

Special Love (verse 21). The Lord Jesus and the Father have a special love for those who show their love by their obedience. Note, love of the Father, not merely of the Creator. Oh, the benediction of the Father's love !

Manifested Presence. Moreover, for those who show their love for the Saviour by keeping His Word and doing His will, there is to be given (a) a special sense of the Saviour's Presence (verse 21), and (b) a special sense of the Indwelling Presence of the Father and the Son (verse 23). This is not merely a blessing for the Jews, but for " any man " (verse 23). After every fresh expression of our love to Him in ready obedience to His revealed will, there comes a fresh realisation of the love and presence of the Father and of the Son.

Christ's Legacy (verse 27). The soldiers got His clothes ; John got His mother ; Joseph of Arimathaea got His body ; His Father got His Spirit ; we may have His peace. The world would have us have peace by ignoring our sin and troubles. Christ's way is by setting our sin before us, and then directing us to the Precious Blood, and then directing our eyes off self unto the Lord. Dr. Payson, when racked with pain, said : " I have great pain, but I have great peace "

FRUITFULNESS

I. ITS DESIRABILITY .. .. verse 2

It is for this the Vine exists, for its wood is of
no use for furniture.

Fruitfulness of Character, rather than in service. The Fruit of the Spirit (Gal. 5.
22, 23). Note also " the fruit of works "
(Psa. 104. 13) ; mouth (Prov. 12. 14 ; Heb.
13. 15) ; thoughts (Jer. 6. 19) ; holiness,
(Rom. 6. 22) ; Spirit (Gal. 5. 22) ; righteousness (Heb. 12. 11).

III. ITS PERIL .. .. vv. 2, 6

IV. ITS CONDITIONS

1. **Purging** (verses 2, 3). Cleansing by the Word.
2. **Abiding in Him** (verse 4). Union Maintained.
3. **His Word Abiding in Us** (verse 7). Meditation.
4. **Continuing in His Love** (verse 9). No spasmodic con-
   secration.
5. **Keeping His Commandments** (verse 10).
6. **Loving One Another** (verse 12).

V. ITS CULTURE

1. **The Cultivator.** (F.F. for " Husbandman.")
2. **His Methods.** The Husbandman is never so near the
   Vine as when He is pruning it.

VI. ITS RESULTS

1. **Enduring Fruit,** .. .. verse 16
2. **Answered Prayers,** .. .. ,, 16
3. **Satisfied Desires,** .. .. ,, 7
4. **God Glorified,** .. .. ,, 8

Says Mr. F. P. Wood : " A friend of mine, who is a clergyman, has in his
study a striking motto. Over his desk are these words, ' *Beware of the
barrenness of a busy life.*' This hints at the dread possibility of being
engaged every moment of our days in His work, and yet being barren."

What a bombshell is verse 5 : " Apart from Me ye can do nothing."
What a verdict on all the good works of unconverted men and women !
What a verdict on all that is done by lives not lived in union with Christ.

Occasion. (1) This was the time for pruning in Palestine, and as our
Lord and His disciples were making their way to Gethsemane they may
have passed some fires where the husbandmen were burning the results
of the pruning.

(2) The vine was a Jewish national emblem, as our Rose, Thistle, or
Shamrock.

(3) It is a significant token of our Lord's calm collectedness that, even
at that supreme and heart-shaking moment, He should have been at
leisure to observe and use for purposes of teaching, such events.

FRIENDSHIP WITH CHRIST

I. ITS REALITY

Horace Bushnell, walking down the streets of Hartford, said to a friend : " I know Jesus Christ better than I know any man in Hartford, and if He were to meet us He would say, ' There comes Horace Bushnell : he is one of My friends.' " Friendship with Him is a very real thing.

II. ITS BLESSEDNESS

John G. Paton, one of the missionaries to the Hebrides, had to dig the grave of his young wife and child, and bury them himself. " But for Jesus," he said, " and the fellowship He vouchsafed me there, I must have gone mad and died beside the lonely grave. All that is possible of sympathy through human friendship can come to a man through the friendship of Christ."

III. ITS UNIQUENESS

He is not merely a Friend to us, but He makes us His friends.

IV. ITS DEVELOPMENT

He must be a Saviour before He can become Friend.

V. ITS PRIVILEGES

1. **Frankness**, to know the reason why (verse 15).
2. **Fellowship**.

VI. ITS OBLIGATIONS

1. **Obedience** (verse 14).
2. **Love.** Obedience is the fruit of love—" Ye will " (R.V. of verse 15).
3. **Reverence.** This is no *ordinary* friendship.
4. **Like-mindedness.** Through regeneration and Bible Study.

THE HOLY SPIRIT

I. HIS NAME .. ..   verse 26

" Comforter " or Helper (M.) ; Advocate (W.).

II. HIS DEITY .. ..   ,, 26

In John 8. 42 the Lord said He Himself proceeded from the Father, and He uses the
same expression here respecting the Holy
Spirit, thus plainly teaching His Deity.

III. HIS PERSONALITY .. ..   ,, 26

" From the Father's presence " (Weymouth),
bringing out His Personality.

IV. HIS MISSION .. ..   ,, 26

A Sent One.

V. HIS BURDEN .. ..   ,, 26

He Speaks of the Lord Jesus, and never draws
attention to Himself. And the more the
Holy Spirit possesses us the more will we
think of the Saviour. To be filled with
the Holy Spirit means to be filled with a
love for the Lord Jesus.

" **If.**" The frequency with which this small word occurs in this section
is very remarkable. He will not startle them by the bare, naked statement
which they, in their depression and agitation were not able to endure
(verse 18).

The Reason why the world will hate them is because they will reveal in
speech and life the Lord Himself (verses 19 to 21).

Comforter. Verse 18 was one of the favourite texts of Melanchthon.
He quotes it frequently with deep feeling after the death of his dear friend
Luther.

" **Ye SEE Me,**" though He would be away.   Not past tense, but present.

" **Advocate.**" A tender, wooing Advocate. Not a hard, cold, blustering
pleader like some legal folk.

MISTAKEN ZEAL

But for the hard facts of history, we could hardly credit
these verses

I. STUMBLING BLOCKS REMOVED .. .. verse 1
"Should not be made to stumble" (R.V.);
"To clear stumbling blocks out of your
paths" (w.).

II. SERVING GOD BY KILLING .. .. ,, 2

III. TRUE REASON FOR WORLD'S ENMITY .. ,, 3

IV. REASON FOR A NEW REVELATION .. ,, 4

The Figure of Speech in verse 1 is that of a path a traveller takes, but
meeting many unforseen obstacles, and having been tripped up quite
unexpectedly many times, at last gives up in despair and retraces his steps.
That is an evil Christ desired to shield His disciples from, so He prepares
them and us by foretelling the dangers.

The Zealots. After our Lord's death this Jewish sect, a kind of Black
Gang, came into existence, who considered the murder of Christians as
service for God, so soon did bitter persecution begin.

In the Talmud we find this : " He who sheds the blood of the ungodly
(and Christians were viewed as such) is equal to him who brings an offering
to God." No bitterness is so dreadful as that which is based upon a
religious conviction, even though it be fanaticism. Many of these perse-
cutors were kind and sympathetic men, but their creed moved them to
dreadful cruelty. What a crushing reply is this to misguided folk who say
it does not matter what we believe, so be that we are sincere.

The True Reason for the World's Enmity (verse 3). If to know Him is
to love Him, not to know Him means to hate Him.

THE SPIRIT AND THE WORLD

I. THREEFOLD WORK
1. **Reprove,** .. .. Chide (A.V.).
2. **Convince,** .. Reason (*margin*).
3. **Convict,** .. .. Conviction (w.).

II. THREEFOLD PROBLEM
1. **Sin,** .. .. Sin of Unbelief.
2. **Righteousness,** .. Satisfied and Established.
3. **Judgment** .. Of Sin at the Cross.

III. THREEFOLD OUTCOME
1. **Sin Discovered.**
2. **Righteousness Secured**
3. **The Cross Visited.**

In Unconverted Hearts. Here the threefold work of the Holy Spirit in the minds and hearts of the unconverted is given. Only the Holy Spirit can produce conviction, and give clear views of saving truth. Oh, that all Christian workers would ever remember this, and ever work in utter dependence upon Him!

For the Believer. Verse 13 gives His work in the hearts and minds of His own dear people.

The Triune God. The Holy Spirit ever speaks in blessed and perfect co-operation with the Father and with the Son (verse 13).

The Glory of the Son. The Holy Spirit never cares to speak of Himself, but of the Lord Jesus (verse 14).

A New Sin. The coming of the Spirit (verse 9) brought into being a new sin, or an old sin in a new light, the light of the Cross.

A Necessary Expediency (verse 7). Also look at John 11. 50; 18. 14; 1 Cor. 6. 12; 10. 23; 2 Cor. 12. 1.

SATISFACTION OF MIND

How the Holy Spirit will end our Questionings (verse 23, R.V.)

I. GROWTH IN GRACE

The Holy Spirit will end our questionings by ending spiritual immaturity. Childhood is age of questions, but when we reach maturity we have solved many problems, and learned that others are not soluble. So, too, in our spiritual lives.

II. QUICKENING MENTAL FACULTIES

The Spirit of God also exerts a wonderful influence upon our reasoning powers.

III. TAUGHT OF THE SPIRIT

Among the things, the Spirit gives us assurance on the following—

1. **Our Standing.**   ..   " Ye in Me."
2. **His Indwelling,**   ..   " I in you."
3. **The Trinity,**   ..   " I am in My Father."
4. **Power of Prayer,**   ..   " Ask and receive " (vv. 23, 24).
5. **Satisfaction,**   ..   " He will give " (verse 23)
6. **Fulness of Joy,**   ..   Verse 24.
7. **The Father's Love.**

Mind and Heart. Yes, a satisfied mind as well as heart; a satisfied mind through the heart and by the Spirit.

Meaning. Our Lord did not mean that He was weary of their questioning, nor that they would cease to ask Him because they would ask some one else. It meant that something would happen that would, at one step, solve their questionings.

"**That Day**" is the clue, the day of the descent of the Holy Ghost. In "That Day," so enlightened would they be that they would no longer seek from Him an explanation of their doubts and fears, because that blessed filling will lead to a speedy satisfaction.

TRIBULATION AND PEACE

I. INEVITABLE TRIBULATION   ..   ..   verse 33

"In the world **ye shall have** tribulation."
Because—

1. **We Belong to Him,**   ..   ..   ,, 18
2. **We are Separated unto Him,** ..   ..   ..   ,, 19
   Our life being a rebuke to the world.
3. **We Reveal Him in Life and Character,**   ..   ,, 20
   And it hates Him.

II. POSSIBLE PEACE   ..   ..   ,, 33

"In Me **ye might have** peace."

1. **Because we are in Christ.** "In Me."
2. **Because we Rest on His Word.** "I have spoken."
3. **Because we are Forewarned,** ..   ..   ..   ,,   1
4. **Because it is an Honour** to suffer for Him,   ..   ,, 20

Why this Warning? "Should not stumble" (chap. 16. 1. R.V.). "Clear stumbling blocks out of your way" (W.).

We Belong to Him. A bully, afraid of tackling a man, can hurt that man more by attacking his children. Satan knows he is touching Christ in His tenderest and most sensitive part when he touches us. "He that toucheth you toucheth the apple of His eye."

Illustration. In the Pitti Palace, Florence, there are two pictures hanging side by side. One represents a stormy sea, with its wild waves, black clouds, and fierce lightning flashing across the sky; in the waters a human face is seen, wearing an expression of the utmost agony and despair.

This is the condition of the one "in the world." The other picture also represents a sea tossed by *as fierce a storm*, with clouds as dark; but out of the midst of the waves a rock rises against which the waves dash in vain. In a cleft of the rock are some tufts of grass and herbage, with sweet flowers; and, amid these, *a bird is seen sitting on her nest, quiet and undisturbed by the wild fury of the storm.* This is a picture of those who, though in the world, and in its fierce storms, are kept in perfect peace because they are also in Christ.

UPLIFTED EYES

What Hinders the Upward Look in Us ?

I. CONSCIOUSNESS OF GUILT   .. Luke 18. 13

Illustrated in the Publican.

II. TREASURE IN WRONG PLACES .. Matt. 6. 20, 21

If our treasure is in the sky we shall
often be found looking there.

III. UNSANCTIFIED STATE   ..   .. Luke 13. 11

Though a daughter of Abraham, she
could not look up.

IV. OVERWHELMING TROUBLE   .. Matt. 26. 39

Even our Lord " fell on His face " in
the Garden.

V. UNWISE WORDS

Observe, it was after He had spoken the many wonderful
words which we have been studying that we find
Him looking up. Oh, that we might never speak
inadvisedly.

This Chapter is the Holy of holies in John's Gospel. Here we must take
off our shoes and tread reverently. Here we have the Great High Priestly
Prayer.

John Knox, during his last illness, was accustomed to hear each day the
17th of John, a chapter of Ephesians, and Isaiah 53. On the last day
of his life (Monday, 24th Nov., 1572) a little after noon, he caused his
wife to read 1 Cor. 15, to whom he said : " Is not that a comfortable
chapter ! " Four hours after, he said : " Go, read where I cast my first
anchor ! " And so she read the 17th of John's Evangel.

The Upward Look. John very seldom depicted the gestures and looks
of our Lord as here. But this was an occasion of which the impression was
indelible, and the upward look could not be passed over.

God Made Man Upright, that is to say, He made him to look upward.
Not like the beasts, which walk with downcast eyes, fixed on earth, where
all their enjoyment is found. To look upward to Him with holy confidence
is our blood-bought right.

FATHER

The Lord taught us to address the Almighty by the name of "Father," for He has become our Father in Christ, and by grace we can look up and use this intimate word. It is—

I. A VITAL RELATIONSHIP

This High Priestly Prayer moves within the realm of His relation to His Father, and thus rests upon the ideal relationship of Father and Son. All true prayer does. "What indeed is prayer but love—love with a want."

II. A NEW RELATIONSHIP

In the Old Testament God is seldom spoken of as Father, and then only with reference to the nation of Israel, and not to individuals. In the Old Testament it stands for a national, not a personal relationship. Even David in his most intimate approaches to the Throne does not address God thus. No one can pass from the Old into the New Testament without being conscious of a change of atmosphere. Between the Books there is a difference, and the whole of the difference is made up by the word Father.

III. A PRIVILEGED RELATIONSHIP

He does not say "*Our* Father." He could never say that, seeing that God is His Father in a sense in which He never could be ours also. Examine verses 1, 5, 11, 21, 24, 25. He taught us to say "*Our* Father." After His resurrection He said, "My Father, and your Father," not our Father (John 20. 17).

IV. A TENDER RELATIONSHIP

What a word this is! It is a word full of music. It is a word with a world of meaning. The longer we know our God the more wonderful and musical the name "Father" becomes. How the heart of God must have been thrilled when the Lord Jesus cried, "Father," for it is a word forming a most powerful argument.

V. A HOLY RELATIONSHIP

"*Holy* Father" (verses 11, 25) is used in special reference to the prayer for preservation from the corruptions of the world.

GLORY

What to Pray for in the Hour of Trial and Sorrow

I. GLORY RESTORED .. .. verse 5

He prays that He, the Son of Man, may be
restored to the position He occupied as
the Son of God, that is, to His pre-
incarnate glory, not for His own glory,
but as His being fitted thereby for completing His work of manifesting His
Father.

II. GLORY BEHELD .. .. „ 24

III. GLORY COMMUNICATED .. .. .. „ 22

1. **By Revealing the Father in His Life and
   Character.** For to make the Father known
   is to make the Father glorious.

2. **By Loving Submission to the Father's Will.**
   Many people find it hard to say, " Thy
   will be done," because they have never
   learned to say, " Father."

3. **By Earnest Petition.**

4. **By Loving Reliance.** How hard He leaned
   upon His Father.

5. **By Accomplishing the Work He was Sent
   to do.**

Only Petition for Himself. " There are many petitions in this chapter
for the people of God, but only one doth Christ present for Himself."
And what was the request ? He prayed not for deliverance from suffering,
but that He might be glorified in and through that suffering in order to
glorify the Father and benefit His people.

" **The Hour.**" The hour of hours. Many hours in the world's history are
memorable, but none ever like this !

Time-Table. One fact we are impressed with is that our Lord's move-
ments were governed by His Father's time-table.

GIFTS FROM GOD

Gifts from the Father and from the Son are Given in this Chapter

I. THE FATHER'S GIFTS

To the Lord Jesus Christ.

1. **Authority,**   ..   ..   verse 2
   - (a) *Over all Mankind*, to rule, control, subdue, restrain, convert, and judge,   ,,
   - (b) *Over your Corrupt State*, in order that He might enrich those given to Him.

2. **Believers.**
   - (a) That He might give them eternal life,   ,,   2
   - (b) That He might manifest to them God's Name, ...   ,,   6
   - (c) That they might keep His Word,   ..   ,,   6
   - (d) That He might pray for them,   ,,   9
   - (e) That they might be kept and be one,   ,, 11
   - (f) That they might have His full joy, .. vv. 12, 13
   - (g) That they might have His glory,   ..   verse 24

3. **Glory,**   ..   ..   ,, 24
   For a study of this, refer to previous lesson.

II. THE SON'S GIFTS

To His Own People.

1. **The Life of God,** ..   ..   verse 2
   - (a) Not be merited, but received.
   - (b) To bestow Eternal Life on lost sinners is the Father's glory.
   - (c) To be the means and channel for its bestowal, the Son's glory.

2. **The Word of God** to nourish the life given,   ..   vv. 8, 14

3. **The Glory of God,** *i.e.*, His beauty of Character and Life, ...   verse 22

4. **The Glory of God**, *i.e.*, Eternal enjoyment in Heaven, ...   ,, 24

King's Almoner. To be a King's Almoner is a glorious office and privilege. The Lord Jesus is the Father's Almoner. He has authority to dispense the Father's gifts.

One Key-word. One of the key-words of this chapter is the word " given " or " gave." In this chapter of 26 verses it is met with no less than 14 times.

LIFE ETERNAL

I. ITS SOURCE

Life eternal is not mere unending existence, but a life of acquaintance with God in Christ. " And in this consists the life of the ages, in knowing Thee " (20 C.). " And this is life eternal, that they get to know Thee " (R.).

II. ITS NATURE

1. **Natural Life** is His Creation.
2. **Spiritual Life** is His Inspiration.
3. **Eternal Life** is His Gift Possessed and Enjoyed in Union with Himself.

III. ITS REASON

" **That** (in order that) they might know Thee," gives us a deeper thought. It will take a whole eternity to discover, and we shall be spending eternity in that quest.

Explanation. In the previous verse He stated that He was empowered to be the King's Almoner, that authority and power had been given to Him in order that He might enrich His own, to give Eternal Life. Now He proceeds to explain this term, Eternal Life.

Jesus Christ. This is the only place where our Lord uses this compound name ; indeed the only place He calls Himself the Christ, and He does so to the Father.

Spiritual Life. Spiritual life is a living relationship to a living Personality. Man lost spiritual life when through sin he was severed from God.

Pray Walking. Has it ever dawned upon you that this wonderful 17th of John, which is *the* Lord's Prayer, was offered as they were walking towards Gethsemane ? Sometimes He prayed kneeling. But He also prayed walking. May we emulate His example. See John 14. 31 ; and 18. 1.

KNOWING GOD

Some of the Results of Knowing God

I. FAITH .. .. Psalm 9. 10
The Knowledge of God begets trust.

II. LIFE .. .. John 17. 3
The Knowledge of God conveys Life.

III. LOVE .. .. Phil. 1. 9
The Knowledge of God produces Love.

IV. STRENGTH .. .. Daniel 11. 32
The Knowledge of God gives Moral
Courage.

V. ENRICHMENT .. .. 2 Peter 1. 1, 3
The Knowledge of God is the Channel of
Spiritual Wealth.

VI. GOD-LIKENESS .. .. .. Col. 3. 10
The Knowledge of God stamps the
Image of God upon Us.

Our Need. " The trouble with us Christians is we do not know our God " (Dr. Andrew Murray).

Men and Angels. " For the unfallen beings the knowledge of God *alone* is sufficient for the enjoyment of Eternal Life. Angels that never fell can possibly enjoy Him in the immediate vision of His glory ; but for sinners and the fallen, there is no knowledge of God but as associated with the knowledge of Jesus Christ." Note verse 3, " *And* Jesus Christ."

How to Get to Know God. First, Approach to Christ (Matt. 11. 27, 28). Second, " Learn God's heart in God's Word ; " love the Word. Third, Quietness before Him (Psa. 46. 10).

An Absolute Knowledge of God is impossible in this life. We ought to be adding to our knowledge of Him day by day as in Eternity.

GLORIFYING GOD

What a Glorious Testimony is this ! How shall we make it
Possible in our Lives ?

I. BY CONFESSION OF CHRIST AS LORD
Phil. 2. 11

II. BY PRAISING HIM
Luke 17. 18 ; Rev. 4. 9 ; Psalm 50. 23

III. BY LIVING FOR HIM
1 Cor. 10. 31

IV. BY EXHIBITING HIM IN LIFE AND CHARACTER
1 Cor. 6. 20

V. BY FRUITFULNESS IN LIFE AND SERVICE
John 15. 8

Past Tense. Note, He speaks in the past tense (" I *have* ") as if His
earthly life were over. Look at verse 12. The R.V. brings out this clearly,
" I glorified Thee."

Our Desire. Do we not long to be able to say this with our blessed Lord
when our life is over ?

His Purpose. We are sent here for this purpose. Man's chief end is to
glorify God.

Glory and Grace. Note how these are connected :
1. " I beseech Thee shew me Thy *glory* " (Exod. 33. 18, 19).
2. The answer being : " I will make all My *goodness* pass before
   thee."
3. " We beheld His glory...full of grace and truth " (John 1. 14).

" **In all Things.**" Have you grasped the full significance of 1 Corinthians
10. 31 ? We are expected to glorify God in dress, deportment, desire.

Only One. There are *many* petitions in this chapter for the people of
God ; but only *one* does Christ present for Himself, and it is in verse 1 of
this chapter.

FINISHED TASKS

Glorifying God in Service by Finishing the Task He Gives

I. WORK ENTRUSTED

He speaks as if His work were ended. It was as good as done, though He had yet to put the crowning touch to what His Father had given Him to do.

II. WORK FINISHED

It is pathetic to note in the memoirs of most great men the "*unfinished tasks*" left behind. The Lord alone could truthfully say, "I have completed My task."

III. WORK WITH A FINISH

He meant more than that He had completed His task. Much work done is not well done ; in other words, it is finished without a finish. But our Lord's work was perfectly done, it needed no supplement.

IV. WORK, GLORIFYING GOD

This is how to glorify God in your work.

1. **Get a Definite Work from God to Do.** We know what our Lord's definite work was to which He so frequently alluded (see John 5. 17, 36 ; 9. 4, etc.). It was the work of—

   (a) *Revealing the Father.*

   (b) *Showing the Way to the Father.*

   (c) *Opening the Way to the Father* by Atoning for Sin.

2. **Do it Perfectly in His Grace and Will.** "I have glorified Thee on the earth, having done perfectly the work " (w.). "I have honoured Thee on earth by completing the work " (20 C.). "I glorified Thee on earth, having accomplished the work " (R.V.).

Does not our Lord's declaration remind us of that cry of triumph on the Cross : "It is finished ? " Glorious consummation.

THE GLORY OF CHRIST

This Verse Closes His Prayer for Himself

I. PRE-EXISTENT GLORY

"The glory I had with Thee **before the world was.**" If His glory was eternal, so was He. Before all worlds our glorious Saviour was associated with the Eternal God in His essential glory.

II. GLORY RESTORED

"Glorify Thou Me."

III. GLORY CROWNED

With the Father's Immediate Presence.

IV. GLORY FROM THE FATHER

"Glorify Thou Me." It is the Father alone who can glorify His Son.

Intimacy of Prayer. Note the change of pronouns in verse 4. Christ began His prayer in the third person : " Glorify Thy Son " (verse 1) ; now He has got to the first : " Glorify Thou Me." Though prayer should begin in the third person, before long we ought to get to the first.

" **Beside.**" The full force of the request in this verse is not seen at first. " With " means " beside," insert that in and it opens up. " And now Father, do Thou glorify Me *in Thine own Presence*, with the glory that I had *in Thy Presence* before the world existed " (W.). " And now do Thou honour Me, Father, *at Thy own side*, with *the honour which I had beside Thee* before the world began " (20 C.) He enjoyed the Father's Presence down here ; but that did not fully satisfy Him, He longed to be in the Father's immediate Presence.

The Answer to our Lord will be found in Acts 3. 13.

Our Lord and His Redeeming Work. It really does matter what are our views of Him. The higher and more worthy our views of Him, the greater will be our appreciation of His salvation.

REVEALING THE FATHER

" I have manifested Thy Name " means more than merely
declaring

I. DECLARING HIS NAME   ..   ..   ..   verse 26

BY THE LIPS.

The new name of Father was something wonderful to proclaim, for it was a new
revelation of God. Our Lord had proclaimed the Name, and it is also our duty
also to proclaim His glories whenever
possible by our lips.

II. MANIFESTING HIS NAME   ..   ..   ..   ,, 6

BY THE LIFE.

1. **Our First Duty is to Manifest** the Name, before
   we declare it. " I have revealed Thy
   perfections " (w.). " I have revealed
   Thee " (20 c.).

2. **Power to Declare** His Name is by manifesting
   it first. The life speaks louder than the
   lips.

3. **To Win Men** for Christ, we must first manifest
   Him in our life, then declare Him by our
   lips. That is how we are to get them out
   of the world : " Out of the world." That
   was how God weaned Abraham from
   idolatry (Acts 7. 2).

III. THY NAME

1. **The Name Signifies God Himself** in all His perfections,
   attributes, and character.

2. **The Old Testament Proclaims His Name.**

3. **Christ Came to Manifest It.**

4. **Christ is the Manifestation of It** as well as the One who
   Manifests the Name.

Why He Declared that Name. Look at verse 26. Here is the secret
and purpose of manifesting His perfections—LOVE.

THE WORLD BLESSED

The world is not now the subject of His prayer, yet indirectly
His thought is for the world who are to be blessed through
His disciples, for whom He is praying.

I. CONTRADICTORY STATEMENTS

1. " I pray not for the world,"   ..   ..   ..   verse 9
    Then has He no interest in the world ?
2. " God so loved the world,"   ..   ..   .. John 3. 16
    Then Christ must have an interest in the
         world as well.

II. THE KEY TO UNITE THEM   ..   .. vv. 20, 21

He was praying for His own, His disciples then,
     and also for those who would believe
     through them, that through His own
     blessing might come to a lost and ruined
     world. " That the world may believe
     that Thou hast sent Me."

III. ELECTION

This is the vital doctrine of election, the
     election of a few for the blessing of all.
     The elect are not called to a sphere of
     exclusion, but to a function of trans-
     mission.

Centres, not Circles. " The elect are not circles, but centres ; heat
centres for radiating gracious influence to remote circumferences, that,
under its warming and softening ministry the ' world may believe.' That
is the way of the Master. He will work upon the frozen streams and rivers
of the world by raising the general temperature from local centres. He
seeks to increase the fervour of those who are His own, and through the
pure and intense flame of their zeal to create an atmosphere in which the
hard frozen indifference of the world shall be changed into wonder, so
that on the cold altar of the heart may be kindled this fire of spiritual
devotion " (Dr. Jowett).

THE LANGUAGE OF LOVE

The Stages of Christian Experience are here Illustrated

I. LANGUAGE OF THE WORLD
What is Mine is my Own.

II. LANGUAGE OF THE REGENERATE
What is Thine is Mine.

III. LANGUAGE OF THE CONSECRATED
What is Mine is Thine.

"**Thine they were**" (verse 6), "**They are Thine**" (verse 9). How strange this sounds ! "They *were* Thine." He gave, yet He still possessed. Verse 10 explains. It is the language of love. The result of oneness of nature and perfection of love between the Father and the Son.

A Powerful Plea. Note verse 9. We must not fail to notice that our Lord makes this a powerful plea in prayer. "After all, I'm only asking Thee to take care of Thine own.'

Our Prayer. We may plead similarly :
1. For ourselves : "I am Thine ; save me " (Psa. 119. 94).
2. For others : They are " Thy people," save them (Exod. 32. 11).

Security. The fact of our belonging to Him gives a blessed sense of security. A lady, who in the days of slavery in the U.S.A., had occasion one time to give a slave a piece of work to do which required him to stand outside the window on a plank that was held by some one inside sitting upon the other end. The man was a little afraid, but said he would go if only his mistress would sit there all the time. The negro's wife was present. "Won't it do if Maundy sits there ? She is your wife, and won't let you fall ! " "No, missis," he replied, " I doant trust Maundy : she's only my wife, and she'll just go and forget, and git up. But you're my mistress, *and I belong to you,* and in course, you're gwine to keep me safe." Possession makes us careful.

THE WORLD

Seventeen times do the words " The World " occur in this chapter, and in relation to the Believers we may group under four headings.

I. OUR ORIGIN .. .. verse 6
1. We were in the world.
2. The world was within us.

II. OUR DELIVERANCE .. .. vv. 14, 16
1. The world cast out of us.
2. When Christ entered into us.

III. OUR ENVIRONMENT .. .. vv. 11, 15
1. Still in the world, though the world is not in us.
2. The world is trying to regain admission.
3. Christ prays that we may be kept and preserved.

IV. OUR MISSION .. .. verse 18
1. Sent into the world by the Lord.
2. Witnessing in the world for the Lord.
3. Living in the world manifesting the Lord.

" **I am no more in the World.**" But He was still alive and in the world ! So short a time had He to remain in the world that He speaks of Himself as already withdrawn from it.

His Own. But He cannot forget His own. There is great tenderness in His prayer. Though about to leave them, He knows they are still to live in the midst of the forces which have rejected and are about to crucify Him.

" **Holy Father** " (verse 11). This is an expression He nowhere else uses. He prayed that they might be kept and preserved from being tainted by the unholy atmosphere of the world they were still moving in, for it is possible to avoid all things labelled " worldly " and yet to remain worldly, steeped through and through with the spirit of the world.

The Answer. This prayer was most certainly answered. The marvel is that they were not lost when they lost His immediate presence. Verily the Father cared for them and kept them.

KEPT

" Keep through Thine own Name." A Suggestive Study taken
from Different Renderings of these Words

I. KEPT BY GOD HIMSELF

" **Keep through Thine own Name** " (A.V.)   A person's
name, according to the Hebrew usage, is the person
himself. So we might paraphrase, " Holy Father,
keep them Thyself."

II. KEPT IN GOD HIMSELF

" **Keep in Thine own Name** " (R.V.).   Kept as in a fortress,
within the enclosing circle of God Himself.

III. KEPT IN THE KNOWLEDGE OF GOD

" **Keep in the knowledge of Thyself** " (20 c.).   He was
anxious that the disciples should not lose the knowledge of the Father that He had given them.   Is
there not also the thought that the knowledge of
God would be their great preservative ?

IV. KEPT TRUE TO GOD

" **Keep true to Thy Name** " (w.).   So living one's life that is
manifesting the Name of God, being kept for His
reputation's sake.

" **Keep through Thine own Name.**" That sounds strange ! If it had
been, " Keep by Thy grace or power " we could have understood it easily.
What a mind He had ! He was talking, not to bairns, else He would have
spoken simply as to a little child. He was speaking to His Father. "Name"
is mentioned four times (see verses 6, 26, 11, and 12).

Language of a True Shepherd. Here we have the language of a true
shepherd. He was leaving them in order to die for them, and He committed them to the care of the Father.

" **For Thy reputation's sake** " is really the significance in some instances
of the well-known phrase, " For Thy Name's sake." God's reputation
is at stake, and depends upon our being kept ones.

CHRIST'S JOY

The Joy of the Lord Jesus Christ was the Joy of—

I. HIS FATHER'S PRESENCE .. John 8. 29 ; 16. 22

II. HIS FATHER'S SMILE .. .. .. Acts 2. 28

III. SUBMISSION TO HIS FATHER'S WILL Luke 10. 21

IV. RULING .. .. Matt. 25. 21

V. OBSERVATION .. .. .. John 15. 11

VI. ANSWERED PRAYER .. John 11. 42 ; 16. 24

VII. SUCCESSFUL SERVICE .. Luke 10. 17 ; 15. 6, 10

When He Spoke of Joy. One of the most remarkable facts connected with out blessed Lord is that, so far as the Sacred Records are concerned, nowhere else does He speak of Joy but whilst on His way to Gethsemane (John 15. 11 ; 17. 13).

Different from World's Joy. His joy must have been altogether unique and different to the world's joy, if it still was with Him in the hour of darkness. If He was joyful now in the time of His greatest sorrow, His former life must have been a life of joy. Hebrews 1. 9 surely proves that He must have been the most joyful of men, though also He truly was THE Man of Sorrows.

His Word and His Joy. Note the connection in this verse of Christ's Word and Christ's Joy. Little faith in God's Word means little joy ; an irreverent critic of the Word cannot know Christ's joy in its fulness ; a neglecter of the Word cannot have His joy. Observe that the only two references to His joy are associated with His Word.

The Word : 1. And Judas, ... verse 12
2. And Joy, ... „ 13
3. And World's Hatred, ... „ 14
4. And Sanctification, ... „ 17

THE WORLD'S HATRED

As there is a close connection between the Word and Joy so, there is an equally close connection between the world and the world's hatred

I. HATRED BECAUSE OF THE WORD

II. THE WORD FOR THE HATED

III. THE PRAYER OF THE HATED CONCERNING THE WORD

"**I have given them Thy Word.**" What a noble testimony When we ministers of the Word come to the end of our days, well will it be if we can give this same testimony.

Reason for Hatred. The Word is not of men, but of God; is not agreeable to carnal reason; destroys boasting in man; and denounces worldly lusts and sin. These disciples had received and were teaching that Word. Here are men despising what they should esteem.

Comfort for the Hated. If people hate us because of our love and use of the Word, the Word gives support when thus hated. Read Psalm 119, verses 42, 50, and 161. How comforting is Luke 6. 22.

A Commendable Prayer. Hated for His dear sake, what kind of prayers should we offer ? Turn to Acts 4. 29. *Fear* would have prayed for *protection*; *passion* would have asked for *retribution* on enemies; all they asked for was boldness to go on declaring the Word the world hated That prayer was answered by a fresh infilling of the gracious Holy Spirit.

OUR SANCTIFICATION

I. ITS AUTHOR .. .. GOD

It is God alone who can sanctify.

II. ITS INSTRUMENT .. .. .. THE WORD

The Divine Instrument is His Word. Often is
this pointed out in Holy Writ, *e.g.*, John
15. 3 ; Eph. 5. 26 ; Psa. 119. 9, etc.

III. ITS NATURE .. .. REAL

" Sanctify them in the Truth," (R.V.), *i.e.*, truly
Let there be no pretence, no make-believe
about it.

"**Sanctify them.**" Then is it possible to be an unsanctified believer ?
They were already disciples, yet He offered this prayer for them.

Negative and Positive. We have considered His request in the negative :
" Keep from the Evil One " (verse 15, R.V.) ; now we have His request in
the positive.

Sanctimonious. There is, of course, a tremendous difference between
sanctimoniousness and sanctity.

Sanctification is one of the great words of the Bible. It is both instantaneous and progressive. Whilst *positionally* every believer is sanctified in
Christ the moment he trusts the Saviour, *experimentally* he may not be
living as a sanctified person. Surely this petition in our Lord's prayer
points out the possibility, in the experimental sense, of unsanctified
disciples.

(For a more complete study of this subject see the author's *Doctrinal
Outlines*.)

THE LORD'S SANCTIFICATION

Our Sanctification was only made possible through that of the Lord Jesus Christ

I. CHRIST WAS SANCTIFIED

1. **By the Father** (John 10. 36). The Father's act is in the past tense, when He set His Son apart for the great work of redemption.

2. **By Himself** (John 17. 19). His act is in the present tense, when He accepted the call of His Father and set Himself apart.

3. **By His People** (1 Peter 3. 15, R.V.). We, too, have to set apart the Christ already in our hearts from common and ordinary uses. He is a " fire-escape," but He desires to be very much more. He longs to hear us say:

> " Thou, O Christ, art all I want ;
> More than all in Thee I find."

II. RESULT OF HIS SANCTIFICATION

Our sanctification was only made possible through Christ's sanctification.

     1. **The Source of Ours**
     2. **The Ground of Ours**
     3. **The Reason of Ours**
     4. **The Measure of Ours**

Meaning. This verse has puzzled many. The clue is the recognition of the threefold meaning of sanctification in the Word.

1. Cleansing of the body and the garments (Exod. 14. 10, 11).

2. Purifying of the heart and mind (2 Cor. 7. 1 ; 1 Thess. 5. 23).

3. The setting apart of the clean for sacred or special use (Eph. 5. 26, R.V.). In other words, to devote, to set aside for a specific purpose. Our Lord Jesus was sanctified in the latter sense.

UNITY

Lessons from Christ's Prayer for Unity

I. THE POSSIBILITY .. .. verse 11
It is to be the issue of God's keeping.

II. THE PATTERN .. .. vv. 11, 21
This is nothing less than a holy fellowship after the pattern of the Divine Unity.

III. THE NATURE
1. **Union of Heart and Soul** (Acts 4. 32).
2. **Union of Mind and Mouth** (1 Cor. 1. 10).

IV. THE BOND .. .. verse 21
" **One in Us.**" When Adam fell, the Lord said, "Behold the man is become as one of us," and so he was driven away from the Tree of Life. But Christ's prayer in John is "that they all may be one in us," and in Revelation man is welcomed back to the Tree of Life, and Christ's prayer is answered.

V. THE OBJECT .. .. vv. 21, 23
1. **That the World may Believe.**
2. **That the World may Know.**

VI. THE PATHWAY
1. **Believe in Me,** .. .. verse 20
2. **His Glory Given,** .. .. ,, 22
3. **Indwelling of Christ,** .. .. ,, 23

Unity and Uniformity. Note the wide difference there is between these two.

The Divisions amongst the evangelicals of to-day are only in a sense like the surface cracks on a dry field, and a few inches down there is continuity and unity.

OUR GLORIOUS FUTURE

I. EXALTED COMPANIONSHIP

"**Be with Me.**" To be with Him is to realise all our highest aspirations.

II. BLESSED OCCUPATION

"**Behold My Glory.**" In verse 22 we have Glory communicated, which qualifies us to behold His Glory. At present we only see it dimly, as in a mirror (2 Cor. 3. 18).

III. PRIVILEGED PARTNERSHIP

We shall be more than mere spectators of His glory, we shall be participators in it.

Two Prayers. "Father, forgive them," is His prayer for those not His. "Father, I will...that they may behold my glory," is His prayer for His own.

His Purpose. Note, He expresses Himself, not in the form of a request, but rather the declaration of a settled purpose. He declared His will because He knew that His will was in perfect harmony with His Father's will. Is it possible for mortal man ever to pray like this, and reverendly to command God ? The biographers of some of God's faithful and loyal servants give instances of such experiences.

"**Where I am.**" He was yet on the earth, yet in Heaven too, for He still possessed in His humiliation the attribute of omnipresence. Have you ever pondered over John 3. 13 ? The Son of Man—Jesus Himself, most certainly was on the earth when He discoursed with Nicodemus, yet He declared He was also "*in* Heaven." Think of Him only as man, and this sentence is foolish ; remember He is the Second Person in Deity, and how reasonable and easily acceptable and understood.

TRUE PREACHING

In this Verse our Lord Expresses the Aim of all True Preaching

I. HIS LOVE DECLARED

" I have declared Thy Name," and this should be our set purpose also, tell of God, and of His love, that that love might take possession of the hearers.

II. HIS LOVE ILLUSTRATED

" The love wherewith Thou hast loved Me." He illustrated in Himself the love of God in order that we might share it.

III. HIS LOVE SHARED

" May be in them, and I in them." The indwelling Christ makes our participation in the Divine Love possible.

The Last Words. This is the solemn and calm close of Christ's great High-Priestly prayer, the very last words He spoke before Gethsemane and Calvary, and these last words were of love ! And the fact that they are the closing words of that most profound prayer invests them with solemn and deep meaning.

" Have " and " Will." Notice the " Have " and the " Will." He has declared God's Name, His last, best name of Love ; but He is still declaring it, He is still the active Teacher of the world.

The Summit. Surely He reached in petition no greater height than this, viz., that His whole people be filled with God's own love.

Illustration. He prays that their hearts may "be the scene and arena of the Divine Love," as an old teacher has put it.

Preacher's Aim. Preachers should ever aim so to tell of God's love that that love might take possession of the hearers.

Observe the R.V. It is wise of all Bible students to keep their eyes on the Revised Version rendering : " Wherewith Thou *lovest* Me," the present, not the past, tense

SECTION **3**

LOVE'S TRIUMPH

JOHN 18—20

CHRIST SACRIFICING HIMSELF FOR ALL AS LOVE

I. Love Tried and Faithful (18—19)

II. Love Triumphant and Forgiving (20)

THE MAJESTY OF CHRIST

Here we have the Lord Jesus in His Majesty as the Terrible One
Why did the Soldiers fall Backward ?

I. HIS GOODNESS AND PURITY
1. **Pure and Calm Natures** have a terror for rude and impure ones.
2. **The Awfulness** of Christ's Purity and Goodness.
3. **They were made Cowards by it.**

II. HIS CALMNESS AND COLLECTEDNESS
1. **They expected Him to hide** away, and brought lanterns to hunt Him (the Light of the World).
2. **He comes forth to meet them.**
3. **With the three words** : "**I am He,**" He struck terror into them, and they lost their nerve.

III. HIS DIVINE MAJESTY AND GLORY
1. **The flashing forth** of hidden Deity.
2. **A temporary, slight drawing aside** of the curtain hiding the uncreated glory.
3. **This, too, would add** to the reason of their falling backward.

The Lion and the Lamb. To John the Lion was as a Lamb (Rev. 5. 4-6) ; to the unsaved, the Lamb is as a Lion. Here we have the Lord Jesus as the Terrible One. If we will not allow Him to be to us, " Gentle Jesus, meek and mild," He will become the Terrible Jesus, majestic and awful.

Only One Record. This remarkable incident is only recorded by John, and fits in with the purpose of the Gospel, the setting forth of the glory of Christ as the Divine One.

Compared with Saul. They fell backward, and not forward, as Saul did (Acts 9. 4).

The Voluntariness of Christ's Death. He voluntarily surrendered Himself to death. It was not their power, but His own pity, which drew Him to the Judgment Hall and the Cross. He did not die because He could not have avoided it, but because He would not.

PETER

I. PETER AT THE FIRE .. .. .. verse 18

Note the steps in Peter's fall—

1. **He Slept,** when he ought to have been praying.
2. **He Followed Afar Off,** when he ought to have been near his Lord.
3. **He Walked into Temptation,** not considering his own weakness.
4. **He Denied his Lord** and blasphemed.

II. PETER IN THE FIRE .. Verses 15-18, 25-27

1. **The Fire of Memory.** Recollection of past blessings.
2. **The Fire of Conscience.** Awakened by the Lord's look.
3. **The Fire of Remorse.** For treating his Lord so badly.

III. PETER ON FIRE .. .. .. Acts 2. 3, 4

1. **The Fire of the Holy Spirit** falling upon him.
2. **He became a changed man.** On fire for his Lord, a consecrated and Christ-centred man.

The Illegality of this Trial can be seen by noting the rule governing trials in the Talmud : " Criminal processes can neither commence nor terminate but during the course of the day. (This trial took place at night.) No kind of judgment is to be executed neither on the eve of the Sabbath, nor the eve of any festival." (This trial took place on the evening of the Feast).

Peter Feeling Cold. Peter was not only suffering from a physical chill (Jerusalem, 2500 feet above the level of the sea, is cold at nights), but also from a spiritual chill. There are various fires men try to warm themselves at these days : The world's fire—worldly pleasures and fame ; the critical fire—where all that is sacred and holy is criticised.

JESUS BEFORE PILATE

I. MERE FORMALISTS .. .. .. ch. 18. 28
They considered they would be defiled by a
Gentile habitation not cleansed from
leaven ; but did not think they were
defiled by condemning innocent blood.

II. A RUDE REPLY .. .. .. ch. 18. 29,30
Pilate asked a sensible question, but received
an insolent reply.

III. REALITY IN RELIGIOUS INQUIRY .. ch. 18. 34
Is this your own question or another's ? Are
you a gabbler or gossiper, or a thinker and
student ? Has some one prompted you,
or is it the product of your own thinking ?

IV. A GREAT CONFESSION .. .. .. ch. 18. 37
When asked a straight question, our Lord gave
Pilate a direct reply, making a great
confession.

V. A CHARACTERISTIC MOOD AND METHOD ch. 18. 38
Pilate asked a question, but did not wait for an
answer. Was it a despairing or a scornful
statement ? Many a questioner is like
this.

VI. THE SILENCE OF THE LORD .. .. ch. 19. 9
The dread possibility of a silent Bible and a
silent Heaven.

The Christian Worker and the Sceptic. A sad change in our times has
been noted, and called the " Dethronement of the Bible." The Holy
Word is considered as no longer speaking with authority. But we must not
scold those who hold such erroneous views, but constantly proclaim the
Authority of the Divine Book, and emulate our Lord's treatment of the
sceptics. He did not treat all alike. Whilst He dealt sternly with the
hypocrite and mere quibblers, He dealt tenderly with the genuine doubter.

MAN'S DEPENDENCE

" No power...except it were given thee from above "

I. NO PHYSICAL POWER

From Him we receive Life and Health.

II. NO MENTAL POWER

Our Brains are His Gift to be Developed and Trained.

III. NO GOVERNMENTAL POWER

The Powers that Be are Ordained of God.

IV. NO SPIRITUAL POWER

Spiritual Power is the Gift of God through His Son by His Holy Spirit.

Keeping Himself Humble. A retired merchant, living in Southport, has hit upon an ingenious plan to keep himself humble and ever in remembrance of his indebtedness to God. Amongst the many elaborately furnished rooms in his costly mansion is one furnished in simple style—sanded floor, old-fashioned hearth-rug, settle, fender, and chairs, a copy of the humble cottage home he first had when he began married life as a labourer. In this room he frequently sits, just to remind himself of his once lowly position, and to keep himself humble before the Lord who has so wonderfully prospered him.

The Christian's Attitude. It is good for Christians to sit frequently before the Lord and recall to mind their once loathsome and degraded condition, giving glory to the One who alone has made them different to others.

Pilate's Boast. Pilate boastfully spoke to our Lord of his power, when He broke silence by a sudden flash of bold rebuke to remind the proud and arrogant Roman Governor and all his tribe in all lands and ages, of every man's utter dependence upon God, that all power is derived from Him, and that its exercise should be guided by His will and used for His purposes.

IN THE MIDST

I. THE ATONING ONE .. .. .. John 19. 18
On the Cross between two sinners, one saved
and the other unsaved.

II. THE SAVING ONE .. .. Zeph. 3.17
1. **Mighty.**
2. **Saving.**
3. **Rejoicing over Thee,** or cooing as a mother
over her babe.
4. **Satisfied in Love.**
5. **Singing.** The last time He sang on earth
is no later than the last conversion.

III. THE BLESSING ONE .. .. Matt. 18. 20
Where two or more are gathered together
in His Name.

IV. THE TEACHING ONE .. .. .. Luke 2. 46
In the midst of teachers, teaching them.

V. THE COMFORTING ONE .. .. Dan. 3. 23-25
Through every fiery trial there is One who
is with His own.

VI. THE COMMISSIONING ONE .. John 20. 19-26
The risen Lord sending forth His servants.

VII. THE SEARCHING ONE .. .. .. Rev. 1. 13
The Glory of the Lord in the midst of His
own.

VIII. THE JUDGING ONE .. .. Rev. 5. 6
The Lamb of God becomes the Judge.

His Perpetual Presence. Some men and women are born leaders of their
fellows. It matters not where they are, instinctively they lead and their
fellows follow. Always head and shoulders above others, always " in the
midst " of any crowd or company. That was and is true of our Lord Jesus.
Always " in the midst."

Its Power. His Presence makes a Church (Rev. 1. 13), and makes a
Heaven (Rev. 5. 6), and is the secret of final perseverance (Psa. 9. 3).

An Idiot's Vision. Up to the day of his death, a poor idiot had not uttered
a rational word, but in his dying hour he opened his eyes in amazement at
what was revealed to his soul by the Holy Spirit, and exclaimed:

I see ! I see!
What do I see !
Three in One, and One in Three,
And all the Three are all for me,
And the Man in the middle He died for me !

THE RAIMENT OF CHRIST

His Earthly Raiment became the property of His executioners. It was but the symbol of His Character as Sacrifice and Priest.

I. SYMBOL OF PURITY

The seamless robe was probably of linen, and therefore a symbol of purity. How perfect was and is His holiness, without a seam or join. Taken off, He was counted unclean and unfit to live, but His inherent purity remained. He was a perfect " Lamb " for sacrifice.

II. THE SACRIFICING HIGH PRIEST

Our Lord was now in the grand office of High Priest, and was about to offer the expiatory victim—Himself—for the sin of the world. The very dress He wore was similar to that of the High Priest on the great day of Atonement.

III. HIS GARMENT MAY BE OURS

His garment of spotless purity can become ours. Only after they had crucified Him were His garments obtainable. Only after we have looked with trust to the Crucified One can His righteousness become ours.

Dr. Stalker thinks that the idea of crucifying human beings was suggested by the practice of nailing up vermin in a kind of revengeful merriment on some exposed place. Be that as it may, it was a cruel method of executing criminals.

The Executioners. Incidentally we learn how many executioners there were, viz., four. " Four parts, to every soldier a part " (verse 23).

Prophecy. The soldiers little knew that they were fulfilling a thousand-year-old prophecy (Psa. 22. 18)

CHRIST'S FINISHED WORK

" It is finished." In this cry we note at least Four Things

I. A SIGH OF RELIEF

What a relief it is when we have completed some arduous task.

II. A SHOUT OF VICTORY

It was the triumphant cry of the Victor who by death vanquished its power.

III. A SIGN TO THE FATHER

He was not afraid to announce to His Father the completion of the task for it had been well and perfectly done.

IV. A PROCLAMATION TO MAN

It gives the assurance that the work of his salvation is accomplished, and he can be sure of acceptance and forgiveness.

His Last Words. We treasure the last words of our loved ones. These form our Lord's last words on the Cross. Only one more cry proceeded from Him.

Before He Died. Of course these are not His last words to us, for He lives, and still speaks.

A Unique Cry. All of us leave tasks half done, and have to go away before the work is completed. But He finished His work.

" **It is Finished.**" What ? Perhaps no one can fully state all the significance of this triumphant exclamation. " His Finished Work " was a sentence dear and familiar to our forefathers, the joy and comfort of their souls. By this phrase they meant that Christ had perfectly accomplished the great work of redemption He had come purposely to do, and as a result God now does not need to be propitiated. Prof. Clow sees in this cry the four things mentioned above.

BLOOD, THEN WATER

It is not without meaning that Blood came before Water.
This is the Divine Order.

I. ATONEMENT BEFORE REGENERATION

" Without shedding of blood is no remission of sin," and
before a soul can be regenerated, the atoning sacrifice
must be made.

II. REGENERATION THROUGH ATONEMENT

In Tabernacle, Altar first, *then* Laver.

III. PARDON BEFORE CLEANSING

We need both pardon and cleansing.   But

" The water cannot cleanse
Before the Blood we feel—
To purge the guilt of all our sins,
And our forgiveness seal."

IV. JUSTIFICATION BEFORE SANCTIFICATION

Romans 5. 5.

V. CLEANSING ALWAYS FOLLOWS THE BLOOD

Water always follows the Blood.   To say that I have been
to the Blood, and yet there is no change of heart and
life, is untrue.   These two always go in company.
Both Atonement (Blood) and Sanctification (Water)
come from Him.

Points of View.   To some this chapter is but a field of blood, a tragedy
of woe, and they turn from it with loathing ; to others the place of death
has become the place of life.   To this chapter those laden with a conscience
of guilt turn and find relief.

For Law concerning verse 31, see Deut. 21. 23

His Legs were Not Broken, and His side was pierced apparently because
of a soldier's whim.   And yet behind it is the Providence of God.

The Broken Heart.   The fact that blood and water proceeded from the
riven side astonished and mystified the onlookers.   This is of interest to
the medical world, as it proves that our Lord died from a ruptured heart.

EASTER

EASTER FAITH can only live on the EASTER SORROW

I. EASTER SORROW AND FAITH

Without the Easter Sorrow (the Cross of the
Lord Jesus Christ) there can never be
Easter Faith (the hope of Immortality).

II. JOSEPH AND NICODEMUS   vv. 38-42

While the Lord lived these disciples had been
unfaithful to their convictions ; but His
death, which terrified and paralysed and
scattered His avowed disciples, seems to
have shamed and stung these two into
courage. At the first they came to Jesus
by night, but at the last they came for
Jesus by day.

III. POWER OF INFLUENCE   verse 6

IV. THE LORD'S NAPKIN   vv. 7, 8

" **Wrapped together in a place by itself** " (verse
7), *i.e.*, rolled or coiled round and round.
It implies that the cloth had been folded
round and round as a turban, and that it
lay still in the form of a turban.   The
linen clothes also lay exactly as they were
when swathed round the body.   The Lord
had passed out of them, not needing to be
loosed as Lazarus.   It was this wonderful
sight that convinced John (verse 8).

V. THE ANGELS   verse 12

" **Sitting** " (verse 12).   They sit in the empty
tomb who stand in the presence of God
(Luke 1. 19 ; Rev. 8. 2).

SUPPOSITION

One of the Great Dangers of To-day is Mere Supposition

I. SUPPOSING HIM TO BE WITH US   .. Luke 2. 44

A Word to Backsliders

1. Not the first time the Lord Jesus has been lost in the City.

2. For a while they were unconscious of their loss.

3. Discovery of the loss leads to sorrow.

4. The lost Christ may be found.

II. SUPPOSING HIM TO BE LESS THAN HE IS   John 20. 15

A Word to those blinded by grief or absorbed in the affairs of this world.

1. **Mary at first failed to recognise Him.** It is possible for grief so to blind our eyes that we fail to see Him ; it is possible to be absorbed with the affairs of the world so as to fail to note His presence.

2. **She made Him out to be less than He was.** " Only a Gardener—delighting to turn over our plans and bury our hopes. Honouring Him only as the One who planted us in His Kingdom, but not as Lover to hold sweet fellowship with us."

III. FOLLY OF HASTY CONCLUSIONS   ..   .. Luke 2. 23

Supposition is worse than doubt. Doubt usually betrays an active mind, whereas supposition is the outcome of laziness or downright carelessness. There is no place whatever for supposition in the spiritual life. " I suppose " may be considered wise in scientific matters, but is entirely uncalled for and disastrous in spiritual things. " I know " is the language of Scripture.

THE DIVINE BROTHERHOOD

I. NOT FOUNDED ON THE INCARNATION

By His incarnation He became bone of our bone and flesh of our flesh ; He, the Eternal Son of God, became our Brother by assuming human nature. But this is a mere natural Brotherhood, whereas the Brotherhood He announces here is of a nobler and grander type.

II. NOT BASED ON MERIT

These men were not even worthy of being called disciples, much less " brethren."

III. FOUNDED ON THE CROSS AND RESURRECTION

1. **Our Lord's First Message** to the disciples was the proclamation of a Divine Brotherhood.

2. **This is the First Time** He called His disciples " Brethren."

3. **The Disciples Never so Called Themselves** until after His Cross and Resurrection.

4. **The Basis of this Exalted Relationship** rests not on the Incarnation, but on the Cross.

5. **Not Until the Cross and Resurrection** did the Lord Jesus make this announcement.

6. **Not Until we Stand on Redemption Ground** can we claim such a relationship.

Erroneous Views. There never was a time when so much was said about the Brotherhood of Man. It has been said that " Jesus proclaimed a brotherhood wide as human life and broad as human need." But that statement needs qualifying. The Brotherhood He proclaimed was of a new and exalted order, very different from the type usually understood.

" **Touch Not.**" " Take not hold of Me " (R.V.). " Cling not to Me " (W.). Lose not a moment, but convey the joyful news to the sad and sorrowing, and, Mary, do not think you will be the loser. I am not going immediately to Heaven, therefore you will have opportunity of seeing Me again.

THE SHUT DOOR

Blessings always follow the " Shut Door "

I. PLENTY EXCHANGED FOR PENURY   2 Kings 4. 1-7

1. **The Widow is a type of the Lord's people,** who, unable to meet all their spiritual obligations, are in a state of religious insolvency.

2. **Thank God, there is a little oil in their possession.** (A little of the Spirit.)

3. **That sad spiritual state ends** with the multiplication of the oil. And how ?

4. **Not by reading good books** or attending conferences, but by shutting the door, and getting alone with God.

II. JOY EXCHANGED FOR SORROW .. John 20. 19-24

1. **Blessing granted when least expected.**

2. **Through a sight of the Lord Himself** when " the doors were shut."

3. **Blessing** of—
   (a) *Peace,* on the ground of sacrifice (after saying " Peace," " He showed them His hands and His side.")
   (b) *Gladness.* " Then were the disciples glad."
   (c) *Commission* to a great service (v. 21).
   (d) *Fresh Anointing* of the Holy Spirit (verse 22).

III. SUCCESS IN CHRISTIAN SERVICE   2 Kings 4. 32-37

What the staff (verse 31)—ritual—could not accomplish, personal contact, with " the shut door," secured.

Have you noticed two shut doors ? First, the sorrowing mother and Elisha had prayer in the lower part of the house (33) ; then " He went up to his own room where the dead body lay.

THE LAST BEATITUDE

The last and greatest of the Beatitudes of our Lord.   Thomas saw and was blessed, for every one who believes is blessed.   Yet his was not the supreme blessing.   They who believe though having not seen are more blessed, because such faith—

I. IS GENUINE AND ROBUST

The real, genuine article.   Seeing is knowing, not believing. Believing results in seeing.

II. HONOURS CHRIST AND HIS WORD

To say we will believe when we see, is telling Him we are not satisfied with the evidence He has already given, evidence He considers quite adequate.   Finney defines faith as " an affectionate confidence in God," and Saphir as " the echo of the Word of God in the soul of man."

III. LEADS TO SIGHT

" I had fainted unless I had believed to see."

IV. LEADS TO BLESSEDNESS

1. **Of Justification** (Rom. 5. 1).
2. **Of Sanctification** (Acts 16. 31).

A Poet's Error.   How often the words of the children's hymn are on our lips and hearts : " I think, when I read that sweet story of old," etc., counting the contemporaries of Christ who were fortunate to see and hear Him as more fortunate than we are.   But this declaration of the Lord corrects that error, showing that the highest blessedness is reserved for us. Bishop Westcott calls this the last and greatest of all the many Bible Beatitudes.

A Plea for Thomas.   Before considering the nature of that blessedness, pity poor Thomas, who has been much misjudged.   His name now is synonymous for doubt and misbelief ; but pray remember he was only asking for the same evidence the others had received.   Instead of scolding, we ought to pity him, because for eight days he had been sad and sorrowful, whilst they had been glad and joyous.   See what Thomas missed by absenting himself from the meeting.

EPILOGUE

FAILURE OF THE EXPERT

They were experienced Fishermen, old hands at the business, yet " they toiled all night and caught nothing "

I. WHY THE FAILURE ?

1. **Not through Inexperience**, for they were experts.
2. **Not through being Out of the Will of God,** for they were in Galilee by Divine appointment (Mark **16. 7 ;** Matt. 28. 10).
3. **Not through Slothfulness.**
4. **Not through the Lord's Absence.**
5. **Not through Discord.**
6. **Not because of Bad Leadership.**

II. A FORGOTTEN FACT

There is a fact often forgotten, that failure and disappointment mingle in the most successful lives. Christian work has often to be done with no results at all apparent to the doer.

III. THE LORD'S TREATMENT

How our Lord treated His weary and discouraged Servants.

1. **His Manifest Presence.** He had been with them all the time, but He now made His presence known.
2. **Spoke Affectionately.** " Children."
3. **Spoke Considerately and Advisedly,** not asking a blunt question.
4. **He Directed Them.** Perhaps from His vantage ground He discerns a shoal where the fishers at sea-level did not. Or perhaps it was a miracle. There is always a " right side " and a wrong side.
5. **He Blessed them with Success.**
6. **He Provided for Them.**

LOVE TO CHRIST

Why three repeated questions ?　There had been a threefold public denial, and there must be public confession

I. LOVE'S SUPREMACY　　　　..　　..　　1 Cor. 13. 13
" The greatest of these is love."

II. LOVE'S MOTIVE
" We love Him because He first loved us."

III. LOVE'S DEGREE
Human or Divine ?　Two Greek words are used here.

1st Query : Do you love Me with Divine love (as God loves) " more than these ? " Peter had previously claimed pre-eminence.

2nd Query : Do you love Me with Divine love, as God loves ? (omitting " more than these ").

3rd Query : Do you love Me with human love, as man loves ? Each time Peter had refused to claim the highest love, and now the Lord takes him at his word.

IV. LOVE'S OUTLET
1. **Service.**　" Feed My Sheep," " Feed My Lambs," " Feed My Growing Sheep."

2. **Sacrifice.**　Verses 18, 19.

Trusted and Loved. Is it a greater compliment to be trusted than loved ? Love is sometimes given to the unworthy, but never trust. As soon as trust finds that it has been misplaced, it dies. Yet love has *the* supremacy. Love to the Lord is the essence of the Christian religion.

Inquisitiveness. In verse 21 we see unwise inquisitiveness corrected. Let there be no hasty conclusions and unbalanced deductions. Take your eyes off others!